Storming the Tulips

by Ronald Sanders

— TRANSLATED & REVISED BY —

HANNIE J. VOYLES

Stonebrook Publishing
Saint Louis, Missouri

A STONEBROOK PUBLISHING BOOK

Edited by Nancy L. Baumann

All poetry by Hannie J. Voyles.

Photo credits:
Photo of Anne Frank used by permission of Getty Images
Photo of the Dossin Barracks courtesy of The Jewish Museum of Deportation
and Resistance, Goswin de Stassartstraat 153, B- 2800 Mechelen,
Phone +32 (0)15 29 06 60
Photo of Hannie J. Voyles courtesy of Nicole Roberts Photography
Photos of Jan van Dam courtesy of Guy van Dam
Photos of the Pinkhof family courtesy of the family
Photos of Asscher family courtesy of Bram Asscher
Photo of Mrs. Joosten-Chotzen courtesy of the family
Photo of Sini Broerse courtesy of Gerrit Oorthuys
All other photos courtesy of Ronald Sanders and the 1st Montessori School,
Amsterdam, the Netherlands

Cover design by Jane Colvin
Interior design by Nancy L. Baumann and Jane Colvin

Library of Congress Control Number: 2011922576
ISBN: 978-0-9830800-0-8

www.stonebrookpublishing.net

PRINTED IN THE UNITED STATES OF AMERICA
10   9   8   7   6   5   4   3   2   1

CHILDREN OF WAR

Like rag dolls they were tossed and turned,
as the land was being bombed and burned.
Most had no chance—or with a little luck,
they escaped while lightning struck.
Forever they carried what had been.
Forever they remained what they had seen.
They outran the night and fled into the day;
got buried in work, and the sweat of their play
still...

    never chasing the storm clouds away.

Acknowledgments

None of us achieves or accomplishes anything alone.

My name may appear on this little book, but this work was made possible only with the help and support of others. Hence, I thank Marie Hart whose belief in this book and commitment to its value enabled me to stick to the job and finish. There were some fits and starts as the translation inevitably pulled me back into the difficulties of my childhood during the war years and the images those memories evoked.

My family, who knows me best, gave me all the support and love— always.

Marleen Heeman in the Netherlands showered me with her enthusiasm in support of the commemoration of the children.

Certainly, Rita Hansen's efforts must be recognized. She chased my errors relentlessly and did what I did not know how to do. She managed to keep smiling when our computer failure caused great frustrations.

Nancy L. Baumann, editor extraordinaire, took the book and made it better.

I am truly grateful because together we take pride in this work, made possible by Ronald Sanders' tireless research, as a tribute to the children who never had the chance to live the lives we embrace.

~Hannie J. Ostendorf Voyles

Special Acknowledgments

Throughout any endeavor that requires sustained support,
we meet those whose assistance set them apart from others:

"The atrocities of the past shall not be forgotten. May the healing continue through the actualization of love."
Jordonna and Michael Dores (Montana)

"As a youngster during WWI and as a young adult during WWII, I shared so many of the fears and the depravities of that time. I remember how we hid in air raid shelters and how the eerie blackouts and the whine and whistle of the exploding V1s and V2s over London made us realize— on our side of the Channel—how the war was affecting people on the continent. No matter where we live may we never forget, for therein lies our future. I honor the work of my lifelong friend, Hannie Voyles."
Nancy D. Tomkins (England)

"I honor my colleague and friend, Hannie Voyles, for working with Ronald Sanders to bring us the stories of the 1st Montessori School children. Hopefully people who read these very personal and moving reflections will grow in understanding, wisdom, and determination to never allow such sorrowful events to be repeated."
Margaret Desmond Hughes (California)

"We celebrate those individuals who have given voice to the echoes of the past. For those who have carried their story to us, you have enriched our lives with your grace, dignity, and love, and we—and the world— are better for your actions. We thank you."
Barbara, Rich, and Molly Meade (California)

"This is dedicated to those who could not be here—those I have come to know and those I never knew."
Carol L. Hardy (Washington State)

"Pupils, teachers, and even schools themselves were wrangled in places during an era which brought us much loss, and a despair which transcends death. Yet this era also fueled a hope that is alive today. This inspiration can be seen in our own children's eyes and the greatest reward comes from knowing that they are already passing it on.

"These thoughts are shared in honor and memory of my grandparents, two teachers who met and married. Moritz Rülf was described as a warm, caring person who was charming, a good speaker, and had a beautiful singing voice. His wife, Erika (Lyon) Rülf, was not only highly respected, but is said to have shown great kindness. These two teachers left an impression on others and impacted generations simply by the way they lived prior to being sent to the concentration camp at Theresienstadt. These are the grandparents I never knew, people who loved children—their own and those at the orphanage they operated in Koln, Germany."
Nir Regev (Missouri)

"I honor all people who work against bigotry and genocide, who work toward mutual respect and peace that we have not yet found. I hope that this book with the stories of the Montessori children will help all of us to make a more gentle and reasonable world possible."
Marie Hart (California)

"Heschel—an existential philosopher—said, 'We were there at the foot of Sinai…' We were all there with you in the Holocaust, we always will have been there, even those yet to be born."
Lennie Gerber and Pearl Berlin (North Carolina)

"I wish to honor Carolyn Toben, a great teacher of nature and of the earth, who generously shares this love with many, many children."
Gay Cheney (North Carolina)

"The impact of war on the person, the family, and the community was so great for so long that we continue to hear the voices of those war years up close and personal. When I heard Hannie tell her story of survival, I realized how important her and other people's stories are. This book, now translated, must reach the world, must serve all of us to remember—and remember well."
Marion Lay (Vancouver, B.C.)
Penny Ballem (Vancouver, B.C.)

All those years and all those fears now resolve…
As we stand and as we wait to commemorate…
we see ourselves—about—within…
we can see; we must begin
to honor all who came before…
I am like you and you're like me.
            TOGETHER
            WE
saw a world no eye should see
which I as yet may not forget.
Hannie J. Ostendorf Voyles

Further, we thank:

Pam Bodnar (California)

Jan Felshin (Florida)

Edrie Ferdun (Florida)

Marie Inman (Arizona)

Tony and Terry Jewett (California)

Nora Paiva (California)

Nancy Pierson (Arizona)

Marie Abu Saba (California)

Marilyn Shatzen (California)

Shirley Smith (California)

Mary K. Wakeman (N. Carolina)

Contents

Storming the Tulips

Introduction
Hannie J. Ostendorf Voyles

I am a Holocaust survivor—one of the lucky ones, if that term could ever be used to describe that ravaged time. Although I avoided the death camps, I did not escape the suffering and loss. I was a schoolgirl and at the time, I lived in the same neighborhood and attended the same school as Anne Frank. She was just a few years older than I was. I remember seeing her on the streets and at school, laughing and playing like ordinary children did before the Nazis invaded our country and stole our neighbors, our friends, our homes, our food, our hope, and our dignity. She was just another student, just another girl, just another child of our community.

Hannie J. Ostendorf in a combined 1st, 2nd, and 3rd grade class at her Montessori school.

Anne Frank in a combined 3rd, 4th, and 5th grade class at her Montessori school.

Like Anne Frank, my sister and I started our education at the 6th Montessori School, but our family moved to a new neighborhood and we were transferred to the 1st Montessori School when I was in the first grade—around the same time that the Frank family went into hiding. Before long, many students in our new school met a similar fate. Like Anne, they simply vanished.

We were little children and could only watch as our friends were first deported to JEWS ONLY schools, and then were rounded up and carted off for extermination. From my own school, 173 students were murdered. Across Europe there were millions more, but I could only understand the loss in terms of my own friends and classmates at the 1st Montessori School.

This book is our story—the children's story—told by those of us who lived out every day of that horrible time. My own memories are recorded in the chapter "Picking Pockets of the Dead." We are the survivors, the children who were bound together by our school, and these many years later, this collection represents our many points of view. It was a complicated time—a time of patriots, loyalists, communists, Nazi sympathizers, Jews, Catholics, and others—and collectively, we represented every group. Each vignette shares a different experience, gives a different perspective of the same events within the same time frame, and reflects not only the child of that time, but their family background and attitudes.

Circumstances were certainly different for each of us. We attended the same school; yet, had different responses to the war that killed so many of our schoolmates. Together, we provide stark insights into the effects of World War II that history books could never approach. Because we were her contemporaries, this book complements Anne Frank's *Diary of a Young Girl* and other works that explain the ravaging effect the war had on the children. Anne's story tells of her sequestered life in The Annex; ours show what life was like on the streets, in hiding, and in the concentration camps.

The book was originally written in Dutch, by Ronald Sanders. I wanted to translate his work because I realized that these telling memories corroborate one another and thereby validate us, the former students of the 1st Montessori School. Further, our stories affirm the memory of each one of us and dispel the notion that children's accounts of events cannot be believed, simply because they are children. I lived on the Beethovenstraat in the heart of the Nazi activity. I lived within a block of the 1st Montessori School and spent a great deal of time on these very streets. I was there to see it—and to remember it.

For a long time I suppressed my memories of the war, like so many children have done. Afterwards, we all needed a new life, yet the long-term effects of war and deprivation, of shame, of shock, of fear—and the overwhelming feeling of loss of family, friends, neighbors—of country and of culture—shaped our entire lives and the adults we were to become. Working on this English translation was a labor of love, for it enabled me to put my own experience in perspective and bring closure to my childhood.

Amsterdam was liberated on May 5, 1945, and four years later I graduated from the Montessori High School. Days later, I left Amsterdam with my mother and sister to come to America. English became the language of the day. The transition from one culture to another—from one decade to another—was immediate. I went to a public college. I got a job. I had to integrate with my new colleagues in order to fit into this new life. Within five years I was married and had a family. I finished my studies in English and Linguistics, and qualified for a faculty position at the California State University. Then, when a new community college was built in Butte County, California, I jumped at the chance to be involved. I applied my considerable Montessori background and interests to this task and was fortunate to be a part of the building of Butte Community College. This was my once-in-a-lifetime opportunity, and I spent the next thirty years loving every working day of my life.

Although absorbed in this career, I never forgot the children—my many classmates and friends—who disappeared, never to be seen again. Those lost children have been with me since childhood, particularly in my later years. When I retired, I returned to Amsterdam to honor their memory by placing a tile at the 1st Montessori School.

I hope this book will serve two purposes. The first is to teach the truth of the Holocaust—always a difficult topic in a curriculum because it is far removed from our contemporary lives and is a story one can scarcely believe. Second, we must keep this history at the forefront of our collective memory, to prevent other individuals or groups from suffering as we did. We are always vulnerable to societal weaknesses; we are not too wise to repeat ourselves.

THE CHILDREN

The children have no monument,
    their lives without renown.
They played the streets of Amsterdam,
then—suddenly—were gone.

    By truck, by train they rumbled on.
    No one saw them go.
    They cried and moaned in pain, in stink,
    in darkness, hunger, none to drink . . .
    They only had the void above,
    they were too late, too lost for love.

    The villagers could smell them as
    those trains kept rumbling by.
    They shrugged and got used to it,
    while the smoke hung in the sky.

    Yellow stars rose to the firmament
    to light the eternal sky.
    Such became their testament
    to do God's bidding permanent
    without ever knowing why.

Swept into the War

Holland or the Netherlands?

The Netherlands is a small country flanked to the north and west by the North Sea, and nearly half the country lies below sea level. The word *nether* means *below*; hence its name *the Netherlands*. The Dutch used windmills to pump water out of the lowlands behind dams and dykes, to create more land. As a result, the names of many towns end with "dam," such as Amsterdam, Rotterdam, and Edam.

The Netherlands consists of twelve provinces, and North Holland and South Holland are two provinces on the west coast. Historically, the sea dominated Dutch life, and major population centers were established where access to it was easy. The Netherlands soon joined existing trade routes as a seafaring and mercantile nation. Utrecht, The Hague, Amsterdam, and Rotterdam—which has the largest harbor in Europe—became known as "Holland," and the people were called "Hollanders."

Over time, the distinction between the two names—Holland and the Netherlands—faded, as the cities mixed with farm and trade. Today the Dutch still differentiate between the two names, but the outside world seems to prefer to call our country "Holland." The Netherlands and Holland are the same country, and both our people and our language are referred to as "Dutch."

The Nazi Storm
An account by Frank Dodd, a 1st Montessori School parent

After the war started in other parts of Europe, life in the Netherlands continued much the same as before, very comfortable and pleasant. Christmas came, and the festive season was celebrated in the same joyful manner as always, but in the early days of 1940, the Dutch became uneasy; it was apparent that things were not as they should be. We heard reports about the activities of the National Socialist Bond (NSB), anti-British propaganda was distributed throughout the country, and a member of the NSB was caught smuggling Dutch military uniforms into Germany. Blackout exercises were ordered, and air-raid shelters began to appear on the streets. On several occasions, rumors spread that the Germans had already crossed into the Netherlands, but we clung to our false sense of security. So things continued until Tuesday, May 7, 1940. I was having lunch with a friend when we heard an announcement that called all military personnel who were on leave or in the reserves to active duty. War seemed imminent.

> The NSB was the National Social Bond—the Dutch Nazi party. Five percent of the Dutch population were members.

I lived near the Amsterdam airport, and when I got home I saw that all the military machines, bombers, and fighters had been positioned near the main highway. Of course this upset the people, and we spontaneously gathered to discuss the changes. Some consoled themselves by saying the Germans wouldn't risk losing their army to the waterlogged fields of the Netherlands, and others thought the Nazis would attack Belgium, but leave the Netherlands alone. Because the next two days were relatively quiet, we slipped back into our peaceful way of life.

At 3:30 a.m. on Friday, May 10, we woke to the pounding of *ack-ack* guns—the Dutch anti-aircraft, ground-to-air artillery. The Germans were invading. Since our family was English, not Dutch, I drove to the

British Consulate in Amsterdam to arrange our passage back to England. When I arrived, I found that the Consulate had been abandoned and I realized we would have to find our own way home.

I spent the rest of that day calling on shipping offices, but although there were several ships in the harbor, no one could muster up a crew. The next morning I heard that the ship 'van Rensselaer' was headed to England. We boarded around 5:00 p.m., and as dusk fell, the ship traversed the North Sea canal and dropped anchor outside the harbor at IJmuiden. Except for the drone of planes and the burst of artillery fire, we spent a fairly peaceful night.

Early Sunday morning, the captain got approval to proceed, but he decided to stay put until later that night when more ships would join ours. Soon we spotted a plane flying toward us from the open sea. It was a German dive-bomber, and we were his target. Panic erupted. Many children were on board, and some thought it would be safer to stay on deck, while others tried to get as low down as they could. Before we could move anywhere, the bombs dropped—but they missed our ship. The plane came back time and again, until it was finally shot down.

At dusk, the other ships moved behind us, and at 2:30 a.m. we set course for the open sea. A few minutes later we were rocked by an enormous explosion. Our ship catapulted into the air and then slammed back down on the water, listing heavily to the starboard side. All the lights were extinguished, and the doors were blown off their hinges. It was dark and we were sinking.

My wife and I grabbed our two children. Because the lifeboats on the starboard side were completely under water, we made the steep climb to the port side where other boats were being lowered. We jumped in one, but before we knew what had happened, we plunged into the open sea. Apparently, the crew had not properly secured the ropes and the lifeboat capsized. We had already decided that if anything should happen, my wife would take care of our two-year-old son and I would look after our daughter, then six. I panicked when I couldn't find my wife in the water, and after about twenty-five minutes my daughter and I were rescued, but not without injury; my foot was mangled in the rescue ship's propeller.

We were lucky—three hours later our family was reunited in an ambulance that took us to a hospital on the Dutch shore we had left the day before. Our children had been unconscious for quite some time, and we were all as black as night, covered in stoke oil from the ship. It took nearly forty-eight hours for the nurses to clean the petrol from our skin. My wife was in shock; she and the children stayed in the hospital for several days, but they kept me much longer. They operated to repair my foot and I was hospitalized from May until September.

Meanwhile, my wife rented a room near the hospital, and after several days she went back to our home to get some fresh clothes. When she got there, she found that ten Nazi airmen had moved in and confiscated all of our belongings. They would not let her into her own home. Because the trunks from our voyage were also lost, we now had no possessions whatsoever.

In July, I was still in the hospital near the harbor when we heard that all English men in the Netherlands had been taken to Gleiwitz, a sub-camp of Auschwitz, for internment. In August, they deported all the English women as well, except for those with small children. On September 9, the Nazis ordered all Jews and foreigners to evacuate the coastal areas. We had twenty-four hours to comply. Since we had lost our home, we had nowhere to go, but I was able to make arrangements to move to a small house about thirty miles from Amsterdam. The following day, I left the hospital, still on crutches.

I had been confined in the hospital for four months, and when I walked outside, I was stunned. The country I had known had changed entirely. The streets and trains were packed with Nazi soldiers, sailors, and airmen who were marching, singing, and roaring out their offensive orders. German signposts, in their detested yellow and black colors, were everywhere, and the walls were plastered with orders and decrees in two languages—German and Dutch. Our hotels and cafes had been taken over by the haughty Wehrmacht.

When we reached the new house, we immediately registered with the local police chief, who turned out to be very pro-British. He promised to help us, if he possibly could. He had orders for me to report to the Germans as soon as I was fully healed, at which time I would make my own journey to Gleiwitz for eventual transport to Auschwitz. If I would lie low, he said he would put off reporting me for as long as he could, and I assured him I would cooperate.

Immediately, life in the Netherlands changed. All political parties and trade unions were dissolved. Other than religious gatherings, no meetings of any kind were allowed. The press could only publish information that was produced by German news agencies. We were forbidden to listen to the British Broadcasting Company (BBC); anyone caught doing so was arrested. English music of any kind was strictly taboo, and the libraries had to surrender their English books. The Germans confiscated the history and geography books from the schools so they could revise them, and they forced the Jewish children into JEWS ONLY schools.

Despite all these restrictions, the Dutch people stood firm, even though the Nazis tried to crush their resolve. The invaders plastered posters all over the country proclaiming that "Germany wins on all fronts," and we had to turn in all of our radios by a certain date. After that, anyone caught with a radio would be shot. Naturally, this frightened the people and the majority obeyed, but the more courageous had radios built into their cupboards and other secret places. They continued to listen to the BBC, and then passed the news on to their countrymen.

Every business, trade, art, and profession was organized into associations under German leadership, including the Association of Bankers, of Insurance Companies, of Shipping Lines, of Engineers, etc. Those who didn't join an Association could not conduct business. They tried to force the doctors and dentists into their own Association, but every one of them refused, so an exception had to be made—otherwise serious consequences would have resulted. When more than 80 percent of those in the Arts refused to be organized, they were forbidden to appear in public. Even worse, when our students refused to join, the Nazis shut down all the universities and they were never opened again during the war.

Then the Nazis called for Dutch volunteers to either go to work in Germany, or in the Netherlands on the Atlantic Wall. It was an attractive offer because, not only would the volunteers earn more money, they would get additional food rations at a time when food was scarce. The weaker citizens couldn't resist, and quite a number left to serve in the Reich. When the Nazis exhausted the pool of volunteers, they started a forced labor campaign. All men between the ages of eighteen and forty had to register for transport to Germany, where they would work in German factories, offices, and on their farms. But the Dutch did not cooperate, so the Germans resorted to the method they used to round up the Jews—street *razzias*. This tactic also failed because people warned one other to stay away from areas where *razzias* were in progress.

After that, the Nazis raided events where young men were likely to congregate, and they arrested everyone within the targeted age group. They went to football matches, race meetings, cinemas, and even to the churches. Those who were arrested were immediately shipped to Germany. In response, men simply stopped attending public places, but soon the hated Nazis found another method to round them up. They would completely surround an entire village, town, or city area, move in during the night, and set a guard every five yards. In the wee hours of the morning, the Green Police and SS made house-to-house searches and arrested every man they could find. Many were captured, although some were lucky enough

> The terms *Green Police* and *Gestapo* are interchangeable. They were the Nazi Secret Police who captured and imprisoned the Jews and other Dutch citizens. The SD was the German intelligence agency, similar to the CIA. Both the Gestapo and the SD were branches of the SS, which was an aggressive military force of the Third Reich.

to find a hiding place. They ran into the woods and crept under shrubs, or climbed trees and stayed there until the search was over. Towards the end of the war, no man under the age of fifty was ever seen on the streets; it was far too dangerous. Despite all these efforts, the Nazis could never master the Dutch people, and they became so bitter that they imposed the death penalty for the slightest offense. It is estimated that more than 50,000 men were executed in the Netherlands during the Nazi occupation.

Make no mistake: the Dutch did not back down. The Dutch Resistance was organized, and they operated with courage, skill, and determination. One department specialized in forged documents, and every single German signature, official marking, and document could be reproduced at will. A private telephone network was established that extended across the Netherlands and, far from being strung underground, it was fixed upon the same poles that carried the German-controlled network. Under the cover of night, members of the Dutch Resistance snuck out to pre-arranged drop zones, despite the curfew, to signal to the Allied pilots who dropped radios, arms, and ammunition. The deliveries even included light machine guns that were distributed throughout the country, and radios that were used to stay in constant contact with the Allies in London. The Dutch Resistance inflicted large-scale sabotage and destroyed enemy lorries, burned buildings containing civil registers, and blew up railway lines. They stole food ration cards so that their members in hiding could eat, and they took care of the Allied crews who were shot down, then returned them safely to their base. The Dutch Resistance conducted a brave, solid underground struggle.

Yet, they could not protect the Dutch from suffering, the worst of which started in September 1944, when the Supreme Allied Command ordered a general railway strike that was intended to cripple the Nazis. Every Dutch railway worker laid down his tools and refused to work. In response, the Nazis cut food rations to an unbelievably low level, fuel was non-existent, and they threatened to starve the entire population if the strikers did not return to work. The railway strike crippled the Germans in terms of their pillage of the Netherlands, and although our entire country suffered for it, the people wholeheartedly supported the strikers and hoped their action would hasten our liberation.

As a result, the winter of 1944 was well nigh indescribable. In October, the Nazis cut off the gas supply, and soon after we lost our electricity. Then there was no water. We had no coal for heat and could only cook if we were lucky enough to beg or steal a little wood. It was a winter without light; we hadn't had candles or lamp oil for several years. Further, we were completely cut off from the outside world because our hidden radios couldn't function without power, and there were no newspapers except for the stenciled Underground editions, which were scarce because of the acute shortage of materials. Postmen only came once every ten to fourteen days, doing their rounds on foot because all the bicycles had been confiscated. And soon we had no food.

By March 1945, all we could get—with or without ration coupons—was a half loaf of bread per week and, very occasionally, two potatoes. The distribution of butter, margarine, meat, milk, and cheese had stopped before Christmas, and we hadn't had jam or syrup since the early part of 1944. There was absolutely nothing to buy, not even an ounce of salt or a bouillon cube—absolutely nothing. The Black Market was very poorly stocked, and the prices were exorbitant. However, we were able to purchase tulip bulbs and sugar beets at a premium, and I was fortunate to get a supply of both. My family ate them all; that's how we survived that winter. Thousands of other people could not fend off starvation or withstand the hardships of that desperately cold winter and they died, only to be buried in rough cloth—or even paper—because there was no wood for coffins. In Amsterdam alone, 23,000 people died that winter. By May 1945, the entire country was at rock bottom and, had the Liberation been delayed much longer, the results would have been catastrophic.

And then it was over. The most achingly beautiful sight occurred on

May 5, 1945, when the Allies sent their Lancaster and Fortress aircraft to the Netherlands. The planes flew overhead, dropped down to rooftop height, and then they opened their bomb doors and threw out food supplies to the starving population. It was Liberation Day, and we wept in gratitude.

Though we were free, our country had been ravaged from tip to toe. Anyone who knew Amsterdam, Rotterdam, or The Hague before the Nazi occupation could not believe that this country could deteriorate to such an extent. Instead of the clean, colorful grooming for which we were previously known, dirt and filth were everywhere, something we would never have tolerated in the old days. Walls were plastered with the remains of German decrees and propaganda, bits of paper blew about, the paint was peeling, and curtains were seldom seen in the windows. The Nazis had cleaned out the factories, and in many workshops there was not one machine or tool left. Farmers had been robbed of their agricultural implements, in addition to their horses and cattle.

There was almost a complete lack of transportation, except for the military vehicles of our liberators, the Canadians. Terribly overcrowded tramcars traveled the streets along with pedestrians and cyclists who clattered along on bare bicycle rims. Outside the Amsterdam station, enormous crowds gathered to board the few available trains. Large numbers of people—businessmen and their wives, farmers, workmen, and girls—stood on the main roads, hitchhiking to some other part of the country. All types of boats were fashioned with improvised seating, and they carried people from one place to another, sailing slowly and peacefully alongside the electric rail line that the Nazis had stripped of its overhead wiring.

Most people looked fairly healthy, but their clothes were tattered and the children were in rags, running barefoot in the streets and begging cigarettes from the Canadians. Although Amsterdam had suffered little damage compared to the bombing of Rotterdam, the streets looked like they had been hit by a peculiar sort of hurricane. In many places they were impassable because the streetcar tracks had been torn up to retrieve the wooden paving blocks that people stole to burn as cooking fuel.

In the Jewish quarter, it seemed that a terrific bombardment had taken place, although that was not the case. Thousands of apartment buildings were reduced to rubble—the homes where the Jews had once lived. When the buildings were empty, everything had been stripped away that could be used for fuel—wooden window frames, doors, cupboards, stairs and, finally, the floorboards and rafters, which resulted in the collapse of entire buildings.

We were in shambles, and it would take years to restore the Netherlands to her glory.

Herding the Jews

Soon after the invasion, the Nazis began to impose restriction after restriction upon the Dutch. Jews could only shop in the afternoons between 3:00 p.m. and 5:00 p.m., and they were forced to wear the yellow Star of David on all their clothing. An 8:00 p.m. curfew was imposed on all citizens; anyone caught on the street after that was arrested. Blackouts steeped Amsterdam in a darkness that was rhythmically pierced by searchlights that swept the sky for Allied planes. An eerie silence hung over the somber city, interrupted only by the stark call of birds. It did not feel like home.

The *razzias*, the rounding up of Jews for transportation and eventual extermination at the death camps, started in 1942. The Beethovenstraat, very near the 1st Montessori School, was one of the central points where the Jews were herded, four hundred at a time, frequently in the middle of the night. *Razzias* were carefully planned and executed. Sometimes the Jews were gathered according to their profession, sometimes alphabetically by last name, and sometimes by their membership in a club or organization.

> The Nazis operated five concentration camps in the Netherlands. Amersfoort and Schoorl were Dutch army camps that existed before the war, and Westerbork was a holding camp where first the Jews, and later other sympathizers, were held before being sent to the death camps in Germany and Poland. The Nazis built two new camps in Ommen and Vught.

There was always a common thread, a theme that linked one victim to another.

Even though the Nazis came every night, it was always somehow unexpected. At 2:00 a.m., a row of streetcars would line up in the Beethovenstraat, waiting to receive their human cargo. When the designated group was finally assembled, the Jews were forced into the streetcars by German police who barked terse commands at them. They even enlisted the youth to assist. Boys wearing special armbands helped children and the elderly to board, then handed them their baggage. The transports went on for weeks: Monday through Friday, always at the same time, always a horror. The Jews were first taken to the National Theatre where they were held until they could be transported to Camp Westerbork, a detention camp in the northeast. From there they were sent to other Nazi concentration camps, often for extermination. A total of 113,000 Jews were captured by the *razzias* and shipped out of the Netherlands—95,000 of them came from Amsterdam.

RAZZIA IN AMSTERDAM

The trucks of terror found us here.
They unloaded their soldiers
in those black boots of fear.
They took the kids and parents.
What were they to do?
I stood there and asked,
"Will they take me too?"
When all were loaded,
their yellow stars in the sun,
I stood very still
at the point of a gun
.... and so we got lost ....
.... our death had begun ....

Timeline of Restrictions

May 10, 1940	The Nazis invade the Netherlands.
May 14, 1940	The Dutch army succumbs to the German invaders.
October 20, 1940	All Jewish businesses are required to register.
November 21, 1940	All Jewish government employees are fired.
January 10, 1941	All Jewish people are required to register with the Census office. Jews are defined as any person who has two Jewish grandparents.
February 1941	The *razzias* begin. The Jewish Council is formed.
February 25, 1941	The Dutch population declares a general strike involving the transit system, the public services, and factories.
Summer 1941	Jews are barred from using public transportation unless they work for the Jewish Council or the Germans. Jews are banned from museums, libraries, public markets, theaters, restaurants, movies, parks, swimming pools, and public assemblies. All Jews are excluded from trade unions, including journalists, actors, and musicians. Jewish doctors and lawyers can only treat other Jews. All Jewish farms are sold. The *razzias* continue.
August 1941	Jewish students are banned from universities and younger students are forced to attend JEWS ONLY schools. All Jewish assets such as bank deposits, cash, securities and valuables are blocked.
September 1941	Signs that say "Forbidden for Jews" are posted in all public places.

October 1941	The *razzias* continue.
November 1941	The Jews are stripped of their citizenship.
November 1941	"Forced labor" camps are set up for the Jews.
January 1942	Jews are no longer allowed to attend public schools and high schools. Jews may no longer drive a car.
March 1942	Jews are forbidden from marrying non-Jews.
May 1942	All Jews over the age of six are required to purchase and wear a yellow star with the word "Jood" inscribed on it, an action sanctioned by the Jewish Council. All jewelry and art collections belonging to Jews are confiscated by the Nazis. Jews cannot own or use telephones. Jews are not allowed to fish.
June 1942	Jews may not play sports. Jews must be off the streets by 8:00 p.m. Jews may not purchase goods in non-Jewish stores.
July 1942	The letter "J" was added to Jewish identity cards. Jewish women may no longer visit beauty salons.
July 17, 1942	The "forced labor" camps in Germany are discovered to be fictitious, and the Jews are transported to Auschwitz-Birkenau concentration camps for extermination.
August 1942	The *razzias* continue, and some Dutch citizens now assist the Nazis in the roundups.
September 24, 1942	A total of 20,000 Jews have been deported from the Netherlands to Auschwitz, and preparations are made to deport the remaining 120,000. Jews are interned in the National Theatre to await transportation to Westerbok before being sent to extermination camps.
October 1942	The *razzias* intensify.

February 1943	All Jewish mail must be routed through the Jewish Council.
March 1943	Non-Jewish students must sign the Student Loyalty Oath (see p. 49) in order to continue their studies.
April 1943	Dutch currency is declared worthless; the people have no money.
May 13, 1943	The entire population must surrender all radio sets.
May 1943	The Nazis order the deportation of all remaining Jews. The *razzias* intensify and include the capture of non-Jews. Martial law is declared for the entire country. An 8:00 p.m. curfew is instituted for all Dutch. A decree is issued for Jewish women to be sterilized.
August 1943	Working hours are expanded from 54 to 72 hours per week.
September 1943	The last Jews in Amsterdam are rounded up.
October 1943	Delivery of gas and electricity is discontinued.
December 1943	All Jews in mixed marriages are sent to labor camps. The "Jewish Problem" is considered solved.
September 1944	All telegraph communications are prohibited. The Dutch commence a railway strike.
Winter 1944 - Spring 1945	The Dutch population is starving and freezing. Many die from lack of food or freeze to death.
May 5, 1945	Liberation Day.

Sifting the Children,
Shuffling the Schools

Every Jew in the Netherlands lived in fear and felt the foreboding presence of the enemy; yet they did their best to shield their children from this reality. But now, just one year later, their children were the target. The Nazis issued an order to separate the Jewish children from their non-Jewish classmates; they could no longer go to school together. It was one of many actions that revealed the true Nazi agenda: to first isolate, then later exterminate, the Jews.

The Dutch officials were under the control of the Germans, and although they had no authority to act on their own, the people still expected them to work on their behalf. On August 16, 1941, the Dutch Secretary-General of Education, Jan van Dam, gave in to the Nazi mandate to separate the students, which ultimately made him responsible for what were often senseless, useless rules and regulations. Van Dam published his decision in an article announcing that JEWS ONLY schools were being formed and that the changes would be expedited for "those children in question," with no exceptions.

The Jewish Council discussed the matter, and some suggested the JEWS ONLY schools should open as early as September 1, a short two weeks later. It was an enormous undertaking. Every school had both Jewish and non-Jewish students, and every child, whether they were Jewish

The Nazis established a Jewish Council so they could enforce their commands regarding the Jewish population. Nazi orders were presented to the Council, who then architected the changes and communicated them to the Jews. The Jewish Council was comprised of prominent men who honestly believed they could help their people, but they actually unwittingly conspired with the Nazis and delivered thousands of Jews directly into their hands.

or not, was placed in a segregated school. Many children had to switch schools, and because the changes were so complex, planning the massive reorganization actually took four weeks, rather than two.

It was a shortsighted plan that spawned unforeseen complications. The Council never considered how the teachers would juggle teaching children from a variety of different schools and grades, or the strain it would cause them, but the Jewish students suffered the most. Because so many JEWS ONLY schools were added, there weren't nearly enough teachers, and the classrooms were overcrowded. The students had to start over, had to get used to a new school, a new teacher, and new classmates. Their schools were often far away, and they had to walk or ride their scooters, sometimes for miles, just to get there. On top of that, they had to make the trip up to four times a day because children ate lunch at home, not at school. Further, the former Montessori students had been accustomed to a free style of learning, but were now thrust into a strict, traditional classroom, for which they were not prepared.

To alleviate the shortage of teachers, many qualified Jews stepped up and taught in the JEWS ONLY schools. It was the least they could do; most of them had already been fired from their previous jobs because, under Nazi rule, they were prohibited from working in their former careers. Amsterdam ended up with twenty-five JEWS ONLY schools, located in the three residential areas where Jews were still allowed to live.

Because they needed time to make necessary administrative adjustments, parents received the following notice:

```
To Parents,
In connection with the decrease of the number
of students, an additional vacation will be
observed on Friday afternoon 19 and Saturday
20 September. School will resume on Monday,
September 22.
```

During these two days, the entire educational system in the Netherlands was turned upside down. Jewish schools were established in former special education facilities. Non-Jewish students were moved to classrooms that had been vacated by Jewish students. According to the 1st Montessori School registration records, thirty-six of our elementary children and nineteen kindergartners were moved to a JEWS ONLY school. Several joined the Montessori preschool on the Daniel Willinksquare, the only Jewish Montessori School. The nearby Dalton School also became a JEWS ONLY elementary school, and a number of our students were sent there. For those older than twelve, the Jewish Lyceum, which was not a Montessori school, was their only option.

Although Montessori schools were now well established, the Germans did not approve of them, and Secretary-General Jan van Dam came to the rescue. To show his support, he enrolled his own sons at the 1st Montessori School and because of his intervention, even the Jewish Montessori School survived, despite the Germans' disdain.

But this small action did little to improve van Dam's reputation. In fact, the Dutch vilified him for approving the segregation of their children, and when the war was over he was ultimately prosecuted as a war criminal. Years later, many came to the conclusion that van Dam had been a weak man and an incompetent leader, rather than a willing accomplice to the Germans. His own son, Guy van Dam, offered a similar perspective on his father and his role during the Nazi occupation.

My Father,
Jan van Dam

The war started on my eighth birthday—May 10, 1940. Back then, my name was Gert-Jan van Dam, and I was a student at the 1st Montessori School, but after the war I changed my name to Guy van Dam. In the summer of 1940, the Germans asked my father to become the Secretary-General of the Department of Education, Science, and Culture. Our own Dutch government had been dissolved by the Nazis, and all the former ministers had fled to England.

My father was a good man; he always tried to do what was best, without thinking of himself. He was much too naive to be a politician. Most of all, he was a thinker and a linguist. He taught German at the University of Amsterdam and was one of the youngest professors in his department. He was, in fact, a leader in his field in what was, back then, a much smaller world.

Jan van Dam

He asked a number of people if he should accept the position and also consulted the professor he'd studied under, who advised Father to follow his own heart. Back in 1940, it was impossible to know how long the war would last, or for that matter, if the Netherlands would be ultimately consumed into Germany. My father was worried that the Germans would try to force their education system on the Dutch, and he was quite opposed to that. Because he had once been a lecturer at the Bonn University in Germany, Father thought he had an understanding of the German mentality, knowledge that he felt was critical for one who would be engaging and negotiating with the Germans. For that reason, on November 27, 1940, he accepted the job.

One of his first conflicts was severe: the Jewish children were to be taken out of their schools. At that point he considered quitting the job, but he knew that if he walked out, he'd be replaced by a member of the NSB. That's why my father didn't quit; he refused to forfeit his position to a Nazi sympathizer.

The plan to exterminate the Jews was not apparent at first, but later Father was able to save nearly six hundred of them, precisely because he understood the German culture. He worked with his friend, S.G. Hirschfeld, the Minister of Economics and Commerce, to arrange for certain Jews and their families to be protected. These two men identified Jews who they thought could be important leaders in the fields of science and culture in Germany, and who could also bring profit to the Netherlands. After convincing the Nazis that these Jews were too valuable to lose, their names were recorded on a protected list. When they were deported to Westerbork, they had special identification that would prevent them from being sent any further. I will never forget my father's outrage when he learned that his Jews had been sent, in error, to the concentration camp at Theresienstadt. Despite the mistake, because of their special status, no German dared to violate their orders of protection, and most of them survived the war with the exception of very few.

Father was not only criticized for his handling of the Jewish children, but also for his position regarding the Student Loyalty Oath. To avoid being deported to forced labor camps in Germany, university students were required to sign the Student Loyalty Oath that pledged that they would, to the best of their knowledge and conscience, never engage in any action against the occupation forces. Father pondered the phrase "to the best of my knowledge and conscience." He used his contacts with the Dutch Resistance to tell the Allies in London that the phrase was a loophole, that even if a student signed the Oath, he or she would not be bound to it if they could NOT act according to their honor and conscience. He wanted students to sign the Oath so they wouldn't be deported, but felt that doing so wouldn't limit them.

Father announced the new ruling on the radio. His message had been pre-recorded, so our whole family listened together. When it was over, he turned to us and said, "I hope they fully understand this in London." Unfortunately, they did not. London opposed the Oath and, because of that, many students refused to sign it and were forced to go into hiding. Father had wanted the students to stay in their universities until they graduated, a plan he construed because he knew that after the war, our country would need every engineer, doctor, professor, and economist available. The universities were barely functional during the war and it was difficult for students to complete their studies, but crucial for them to persevere. Father worried that if our laboratories, libraries, and the like couldn't continue because of a lack of qualified personnel, these institutions would end up in Germany, which would have been a national disaster.

Although he was unsuccessful in this effort, to his credit he was 100 percent successful in preserving our culture. He persuaded the Germans that all of our Dutch art treasures should remain in the Netherlands, and the Germans honored this agreement. To my knowledge, not a single painting from a Dutch museum ever left the country! Some pieces that were from private collections or stolen from Jewish homes were, however, sold to Germans, but he had no control over those actions. Today, we know that Goebbels and Goering were behind the plundering of Jewish property, and nobody could have stopped that.

Special bunkers were built for the paintings and other objets d'art, and they were labeled in several languages to indicate that they weren't ordinary shelters, they were for *art* and were to be respected by all troops that were fighting in the area, an unbelievable feat, given the nature of war. One such bunker was located on the Hoge Veluwe—a Dutch

National Park—where the contents of the Kröller-Müller museum were stored. I remember going there with my father, and he placed one of the Dutch masterpieces on a chair and explained it to me in detail.

Although his preservation of art was an enormous accomplishment, it could not shield my father from the backlash of the angry Dutch. After the war, he was imprisoned for being a Nazi sympathizer and was charged with aiding and abetting the enemy. He was arrested on May 12, 1945, just one week after the Liberation, and was held for three months without any outside contact. For years he was imprisoned, as they tried to collect sufficient evidence to convict him of war crimes, and even though they found nothing, they kept searching.

He finally came to trial in October 1948, over three years after his arrest. His was one of the last cases to be prosecuted, and his sentence was returned the following month: seven years in prison. Then came the surprise. The court reduced his sentence by one year, and then gave him an even further reduction for good behavior, which meant he would only be imprisoned for six more months. If they had given him one year less, he would have already been free; however, that would have been a blow to the Court that had saved his case for last, just to showcase the proceedings.

Of course, Jan van Dam could have made other choices during his tenure as Secretary-General. He could have obstructed the Nazi effort or even quit. He certainly thought about those options, but inevitably he came to the conclusion that he was the best person for the job and could potentially massage or even alter the outcome. It would have been far better for him and our family if he had thrown in the towel the moment that things started going too far. It would have saved him a lot of hardship, but would it have been better for the Netherlands?

The 1st Montessori School Connection

Today Montessori schools are widely known as a viable alternative to early elementary school education. Radically different from the traditional classroom, Montessori classes group three grades together and rely on the students to help each other learn. The emphasis is on consensus-building and personal responsibility. Students progress at their own pace, and

The 1st Montessori School

they benefit from sensory and kinetic learning, especially in the early grades. If a student slams a door, they go back and practice closing the door quietly until they perfect it. They learn to write by tracing sandpaper letters and numbers and are soon proficient writers. The classrooms have desks, but no regimented rows. Instead, the children group their own desks together and have the freedom to change groupings as they choose, but this does not mean there is no order in the classroom. To the contrary, Montessori classes are known for their peaceful learning environment.

In most countries, these schools are private, rather than public, institutions. Montessori as a form of public education had its start in Amsterdam in 1925. As the city expanded and as new neighborhoods grew, several pilot Montessori classes were approved as a new educational alternative.

By 1930, the population in Amsterdam began shifting from the city center to the suburbs. The new neighborhood in "Old South Amsterdam" attracted an educated people who represented a variety of professions and businesses, and many of the residents were Jewish. In these affluent suburbs, the parents were intrigued by the new educational approach, and the match between the new neighborhood and Montessori classes proved successful. The first public Montessori school opened on October 27, 1927, and was appropriately named the 1st Montessori School. Subsequent schools were named in sequential order.

However, the Dutch weren't the only ones who moved to this new neighborhood. When Hitler became Chancellor of Germany in 1933, many German Jews escaped the regime and fled to the Netherlands. There was plenty of room in this area, partly because it was more expensive than the older neighborhoods and was, therefore, less populated. Many of Germany's Jews found their way here.

Like any school, the 1st Montessori School was the heartbeat of the neighborhood. As such, it was central to what transpired during those terrible years of the Second World War. In 1943, when the quality and availability of food began to deteriorate, the administration was deeply concerned about their students' health and offered whatever assistance they could. More and more children were turning to the city soup kitchens where food was served to the starving population. Determined to supplement their nutrition, the principal sent the following note to their parents:

As you may well know, the children in grades one through four receive Vitamin D pills at school. They receive these at no cost, once every two weeks. Unless we hear differently, we shall continue this practice.

As the war progressed, the food supply dwindled even further. At the beginning of the war, the children had enjoyed an annual ritual

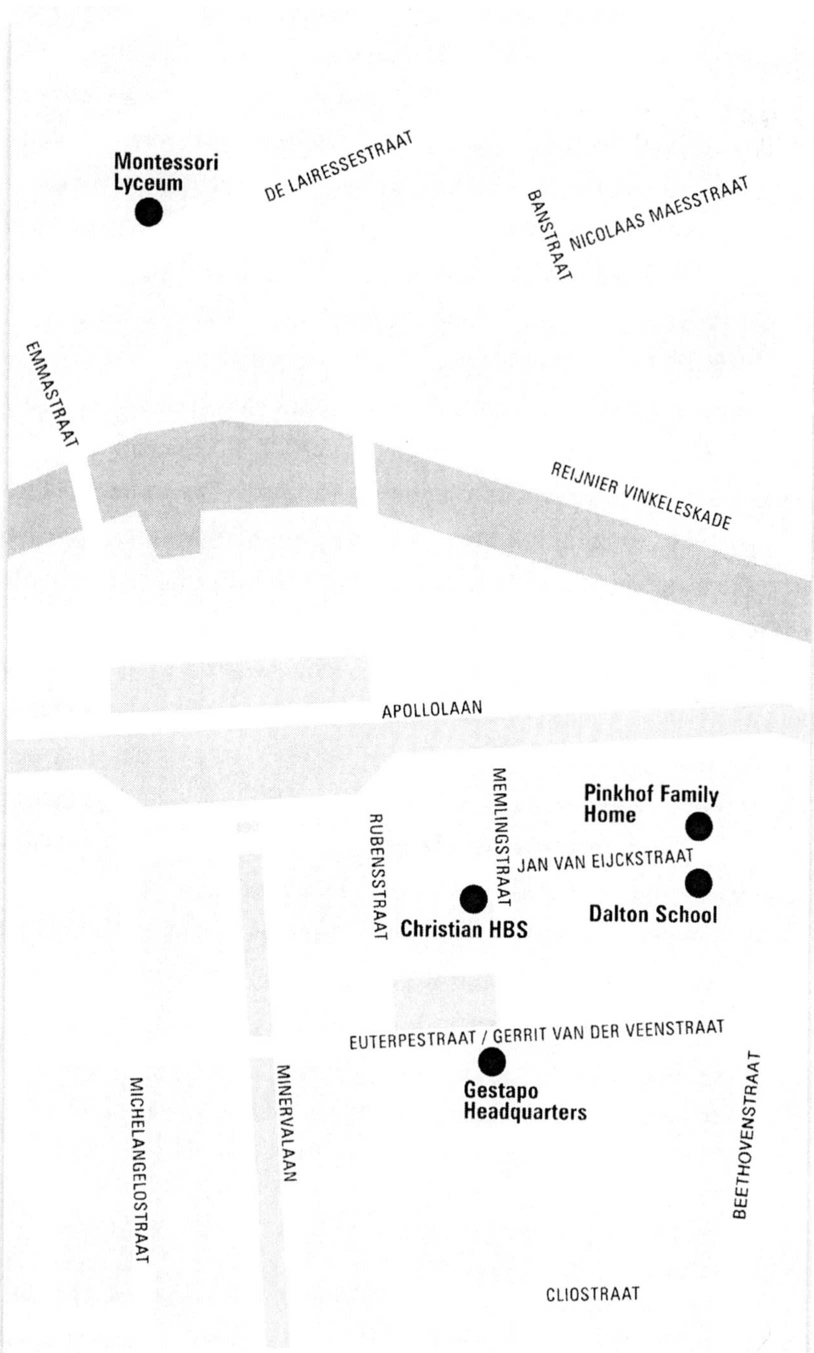

Montessori
Lyceum
●

DE LAIRESSESTRAAT

BANSTRAAT

NICOLAAS MAESSTRAAT

EMMASTRAAT

REIJNIER VINKELESKADE

APOLLOLAAN

MEMLINGSTRAAT

RUBENSSTRAAT

Pinkhof Family
Home
●

JAN VAN EIJCKSTRAAT

Christian HBS
●

Dalton School
●

EUTERPESTRAAT / GERRIT VAN DER VEENSTRAAT

Gestapo
Headquarters
●

MICHELANGELOSTRAAT

MINERVALAAN

BEETHOVENSTRAAT

CLIOSTRAAT

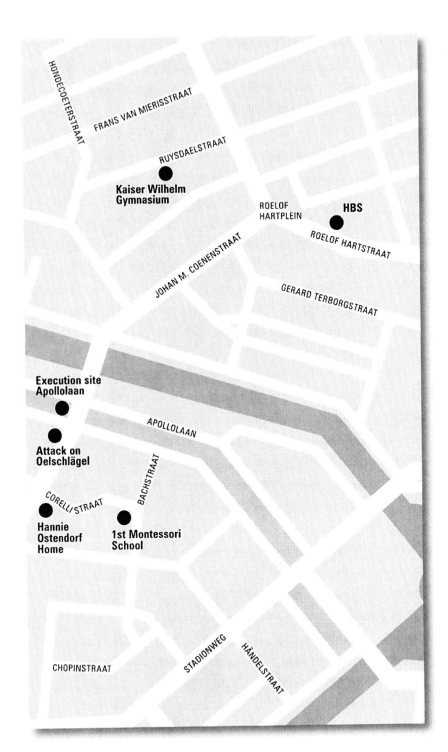

HONDECOETERSTRAAT

FRANS VAN MIERISSTRAAT

RUYSDAELSTRAAT

Kaiser Wilhelm Gymnasium

ROELOF HARTPLEIN

HBS

ROELOF HARTSTRAAT

JOHAN M. COENENSTRAAT

GERARD TERBORGSTRAAT

Execution site Apollolaan

APOLLOLAAN

Attack on Oelschlägel

BACHSTRAAT

CORELLISTRAAT

Hannie Ostendorf Home

1st Montessori School

CHOPINSTRAAT

STADIONWEG

HÄNDELSTRAAT

where they purchased tulip bulbs at school, then took them home to plant. The next spring, they brought them back to school in full flower for a classroom exhibit. By the end of the war, the children were so hungry that, rather than plant the bulbs at home, they fried them and ate them.

The Nazis commandeered most public facilities and the 1st Montessori School was no exception. In May 1943, they ordered the Dutch to turn in all their radios, so they couldn't listen to the BBC to get reports on the war, particularly the German losses. The neighbors brought their radios to the school gym where the Nazis received and catalogued the collection; anyone caught with a radio after that was sent to a concentration camp, and some were even shot. The Nazis also collected copper wares, which were melted down and used to manufacture German weapons and ammunition. The school gym became a warehouse of collected goods, all stolen from the people.

Other schools were also pressed into Nazi service. The Amsterdam High School for Girls was taken over by the Sicherheits Dienst, the Nazi intelligence agency frequently called the SD. It was used for many purposes, including the interrogation, torture, and imprisonment of Dutch citizens who had been arrested and were awaiting deportation to concentration camps. Directly across the street was the Christian High School that became the Department of Registration, Removal, and Displacement. It was the Nazi center for all Jewish Affairs, where all records regarding the Jews were stored, and where the *razzias* and deportations were planned. In a bold move, the Dutch Resistance begged the Allies to bomb both these schools to end the brutality, but they refused the request a number of times because the area was densely populated with families and children. Finally, Prince Bernhard, Queen Wilhelmina's son-in-law, intervened and the perilous request was approved with one caveat: the bombing had to take place on a Sunday when schools were not in session and the children were likely to be at home.

On November 26, 1944, British fighter planes dropped their bombs on the Gestapo headquarters at precisely 1:25 p.m. Though badly damaged, the building was not entirely destroyed, but the Christian High School, where the *razzias* were organized and implemented, was flattened. A grenade hit the Conservatory; elsewhere, bombs had fallen but failed to explode, and bullets pierced the roof of the 1st Montessori School and lodged in the second floor hallway. As feared, many nearby buildings and homes were destroyed and others caught fire and burned. Then the British planes came back to gun down the Germans who ran into the streets, fleeing the burning buildings. Many people died, including civilians and a large number of Nazis who were assigned to these facilities. It was a grievous setback for the Nazis, but the German High Command soon moved to a new location where they continued their hateful activities. That entire winter, the clock on the tower was frozen at 1:25 p.m., the exact moment when the high school was hit.

After the bombing, the 1st Montessori School was closed for the remainder of the war. Without building materials, the holes in the roof couldn't be repaired, and there was no coal or electricity, no heat or light. Even so, some classes continued in the homes of students or in a room in a commercial building or store, with one exception—the principal continued to teach in his office.

Although the school was not fit for students, after the Liberation the Canadians used it as a detention area for Dutch Nazi sympathizers and members of the NSB, along with others who had profited from the Nazi occupation. The school was reopened to students in the fall of 1945, after necessary renovations and repairs were made, including the removal of the heavy locks that had imprisoned the Dutch war criminals.

The war inflicted unspeakable damage. Jewish children had been plucked from their school, families were ripped apart, and friends were forever separated. Of the fifty-five Jewish children taken from the 1st Montessori school, only thirty-nine of them survived the war. Sixteen lost their lives, and one died immediately after the war. Only the very youngest ever returned to the school; most of them were high school-aged by the time the war was over. The children who had either survived the camps or been in hiding came back to find their homes occupied by others, their belongings gone, and their claims denied. Some had lost their parents and were sent away—again—to family members who lived elsewhere.

Of all the children who ever attended the 1st Montessori School since its opening in 1925, 173 of them died during the war. Yet, miraculously, some managed to survive or even escape.

The Ones Who Vanished

The Exodus Begins

The Netherlands was home to a number of British citizens, and immediately after the invasion, many of them tried to escape to England. The fortunate ones from the British Embassy were taken to Ijmuiden, the harbor outside of Amsterdam, where they boarded a cattle transport bound for Harwich, the nearest English port across the North Sea. One of our students, Michael Staal, was on board. The ship stole out of the harbor in the dead of night and, although there was a German patrol boat nearby, it didn't notice them, and they reached the English coast without incident.

Others weren't so fortunate, like the cargo ship van Rensselaer that plowed into an underwater mine and sunk. Yet, on May 12, 1940, the same day the van Rensselaer set sail, one of 1st Montessori's French families managed to escape. Mr. Raphael was the French consul and he gained passage on a cargo ship with his wife and three children. They successfully crossed the English Channel and, from England, they made their way home to France.

Foreigners weren't the only ones who tried to get out. Dutch citizens attempted to escape as well, particularly the Jews, and they found friends and strangers to help them, such as the fishing fleet in Ijmuiden. The fishermen loaded all their boats and were poised to transport a number of Jews out of the country. Former student Eddy Konijn was on board the first boat, but as soon as they set sail, the Germans torpedoed their ship and disabled it. Fortunately, Eddy was able to swim back to safety. The other fishing boats, loaded with refugees and ready to go, didn't dare follow. They stayed in the harbor and the families disembarked, returning to Amsterdam with their hopes dashed.

After the invasion, all the schools were closed for nearly two weeks.

By May 20, just ten days later, the children were back in school and the Nazis occupied the land. From that point forward, they took over every part of our lives, even our schools.

The Suicide Pact:
The Pinkhof Family

As time passed, it became obvious that the Nazis not only planned to segregate the Jews, but to annihilate them. Thousands of Jewish children and their families were rounded up in the *razzias* and taken away. Because so many Jews had been deported to concentration camps in 1942 and 1943, the Jewish schools completely closed down, simply because they had no students. Other Jews who were in hiding were frequently betrayed, and most of them ended up in the extermination camps at Auschwitz or Sobibor, where they were sent to the gas chambers the same day they arrived. However, a few of the children were assigned to work stations at the camps and were forced into horrendous duties. Almost all of them died from exhaustion or were executed; the few who survived had lived through hell.

The parents of 1st Montessori students Herman, Rebecca, and Adele Pinkhof chose to avoid this fate altogether. Every day they watched as their friends and neighbors were torn from their homes and sent off to the camps, their homes ransacked and their possessions confiscated. The Nazis had commandeered Dutch buildings and institutions, and the people watched as the fabric of society unraveled. The Pinkhofs wrote to their extended family about the atrocities and said they knew what awaited them in the death camps. They had little hope of escape, and on

The Pinkhof Family, 1935

September 17, 1942, they committed suicide as a family. Apparently, they turned on the gas and breathed it in until they died, their only hope to bypass the Nazi cruelty that would have led to their inevitable death. Not one of them survived.

First Montessori School student Hannie Ostendorf was the first to find them. She walked to school with Rebecca every morning, and when she got to their house, she knocked on the door. When no one answered, Hannie went inside and, instead of finding her friend, she found five dead bodies. She ran straight to school and didn't tell anyone what she had seen—she didn't dare. Her own mother was a Jew in hiding, and Hannie couldn't risk being questioned by the police.

The Pinkhof family was buried at the Jewish cemetery in the village of Muiderberg. The three children rest between their parents.

Saved by my Dog:
David van Huiden

Before the war, my sister Josephine and I both attended the 1st Montessori School, and in 1936, I was a kindergartner.

Our father had died before I was born, and when our mother remarried in 1938, we had to move to a new neighborhood. It was hard for my sister and me. We liked our former school and our old friends. Our stepfather was working as a clerk at City Hall, but soon after we moved, he was fired because Jews could no longer hold government jobs. We had a rough time financially, and mother went back to work as a pharmacist's assistant.

In 1941, we had to change schools again to go to a JEWS ONLY school. The *razzias* were in full swing by this time, and every day, fewer and fewer students came to class. When I was eleven, I lost my two best friends. Leo Eigenfeld, who had started at 1st Montessori with me, invited me to play at his house after school. That afternoon, I rang his doorbell, but no one answered. I rang again … and again. Then the

neighbors came out and told me that the Nazis had come in the middle of the night and forced the family on a transport to Westerbork, the camp where they held the Jews before sending them to Auschwitz. On another occasion, my friend Wilco

Josephine van Huiden and a friend at school

van Duyvenbode and I had made plans to do our homework together. When I got to his front door, there was a note tacked on it that warned: FORBIDDEN FOR JEWS. His whole family had vanished and the

Nazis had taken over their home. I left in tears, certain I would never see my friend again.

We were next. On June 20, 1943, we were herded onto our own streetcar: destination Westerbork. My parents had anticipated our arrest and had made a plan for me to escape. They prearranged with our non-Jewish neighbors that, when the Nazis came for us, I would simply walk away with our German Shepherd and go straight to their house. That day had arrived, and I followed the exacting plan. I ripped the yellow star from my clothing and walked straight through the blockade with my dog. I told the soldiers that he "needed to do his business." The Nazis loved German Shepherds, of course, so they let me pass without incident. Mother had left some of my clothes with the neighbors, but when I went to get them the next day, they claimed they had nothing of mine and didn't know about our plan. They told me I'd better get out of there before they called the Gestapo.

I finally got help from a Dutch Resistance group who helped children without identity papers. They moved me to Friesland, a province in the northern part of the Netherlands, where they changed my name. I became Paul van Essen, an orphan from the bombed-out city of Rotterdam whose family had died during the raid. I was thankful that no one ever asked me any questions about the bombing because I could not have answered them. The only thing I knew about Rotterdam was the names of two streets—the Coolsingel and the Blaak—and I only learned that from playing Monopoly!

The Dutch Resistance moved me around, hiding me in different safe houses all around Friesland. Sometimes I lived with farmers and, toward the end of the war, I lived in the capital city of Leeuwarden where I attended the Christian vocational high school. Every Sunday I went to church with my host family, both mornings and evenings. Only the school principal knew my real identity. However, a doctor who treated a serious infection of my fingers immediately realized that I was Jewish. The local minister got involved and, God bless him, he threatened the doctor so that he would keep his mouth shut.

On April 15, 1945, the Canadians liberated Friesland, although the rest of the Netherlands was still occupied. After that, I fully expected my family to return from the "work" camps. I waited for them for months, faithfully listening to radio reports that announced the names of those who had returned. As 1945 drew to a close, I realized that my parents and my sister were never coming back, and that I would have to go through life alone. I was only fourteen years old. Later, the Red Cross sent me an official notice that my whole family had died in the Sobibor gas chambers on July 2, 1943—on my twelfth birthday.

I never celebrated my birthday again.

From Nazi Darling to Starving Prisoner:
Inge Preuss

I was born a blonde-haired, blue-eyed Jewish girl in Berlin, Germany, on February 26, 1928. My parents divorced shortly after my birth, and I lived with my mother who worked as an attorney and translator. She hired a babysitter to take care of me while she was at work, and when I was three years old, I entered preschool.

Soon after that, the Nazis sponsored a contest to find "the most Germanic looking preschooler." Who would have guessed that I would win? It was absurd, of course, because even though I had blonde hair and blue eyes, I was a Jew. Because of the publicity, my mother feared the Nazis would discover my dangerous secret, so she whisked me off to the Netherlands to live with distant relatives. These Orthodox Jews were caring people, but it was difficult for me to meet their expectations and their many demands. My family had not been religious, so I didn't know the rituals and customs, nor did I understand the strict Orthodox life. On top of that, I was only five years old and I ached from the loss of my mother. After several months, they put me in an Orthodox Jewish

> Formal education in the Netherlands starts early. Children start preschool at age three, enter kindergarten at age four or five, then continue in elementary school through the sixth grade. The Netherlands has no Junior High or Middle School. At the end of elementary school, students are tested for aptitude and, based on their test results, they are either eligible for university prep schools or for vocational high schools that are less demanding, but don't lead to a university education. Students attend vocational schools for four years, then move on to apprenticeships.
>
> The HBS, the Lyceum, and the Gymnasium are all university prep schools. The HBS, literally the "high commoner's school" is a five-year school. The Gymnasium requires students to study Latin and Greek, in addition to everything else. The Lyceum is a combination of the two, where students study four additional foreign languages. Both the Lyceum and Gymnasium are six-year schools.

orphanage in Leiden, several miles outside Amsterdam. Life became even more difficult; I felt like a prisoner. Thankfully, nine months later my mother moved to Amsterdam and we were reunited. She opened her own legal practice and, in 1934, I started at the Open Air School. In this new design, classes were held outside on the balconies of the building, hoping to prevent the spread of tuberculosis, a prevalent and deadly disease at that time. The environment did not agree with me and, before long, I got really sick, so my mother enrolled me at the 1st Montessori School. On October 1, 1934, I started the first grade.

In 1940, I was ready to go to high school, but my mother was appointed to be the legal adjudicator for the Department of Fisheries and Agriculture in The Hague, and we moved to Wassenaar, near the coast. Soon after, all the Jews were fired from their jobs, so Mother starting working for the Dutch Resistance, doing translation work for the Dutch Ministry that had fled to England.

The first year of the Nazi occupation was a time of rapid change, and it wasn't long before we, considered enemy Jews, had to evacuate the coastal areas. We moved inland to Gouda, where I attended the local HBS for a couple of months, but that also became too dangerous for a Jew. I missed going to school, and I wanted to learn so badly that I took a math class every week from a Jewish architect who lived in Reeswijk, eight miles away. Jews couldn't use public transportation, but I was so determined to learn that I walked the eight miles to his class and the eight miles back—until his family was deported to a concentration camp.

Mother worked hard, and every night a courier from the Dutch Resistance came to collect her translations. This worker, a woman, managed to pass the information to England and, in turn, brought my mother more material to translate. She worked at night and slept during the day, which eventually drew unwanted attention from our neighbors, so we moved to a street where all the houses were alike and we could have a measure of anonymity. During most of the war years, I did all the housework. That is, I did it as well as one could expect a teenager to do!

Every Jew had to find a way to survive the Nazi occupation, and my mother and I had the opportunity to qualify for the Calmeyer list, a list that, according to the Nazi's racial specifications, determined whether you were Jewish or Aryan. If we qualified for the list, we would be declared Aryan and would be protected from the fate of the Jews. Because I had won that contest in preschool, we were hopeful.

Every candidate was intimately inspected from head to toe, and every physical characteristic was carefully noted, measured, and evaluated. They inspected our noses, our earlobes, our eye color, our hair, and even our pubic hair—and then they compared our features to German samples. It was the kind of examination that would normally create shame and humiliation in a teenager, but for me, it was a lifeline. They could not determine that my mother and I were Jews, so we were included on the Calmeyer list and given the precious Aryan status. Now we could ignore the Jewish rules and regulations, and we immediately ripped those awful yellow stars from our clothes.

But that wasn't the end of it. The Nazis took over everything, and toward the end of 1943, a German soldier was assigned quarters in our house. Fortunately, he was not fully committed to the Nazis; he had the lowly job of polishing the officers' boots. Then an NSB city clerk named Jan Boot commandeered our entire lower floor and had us arrested on the suspicion of being Jewish. We were taken to the women's prison in Rotterdam, but thanks to our legal Aryan status, they set us free several weeks later. While we were gone, Jan Boot had taken over our entire house, so we settled in Utrecht, where my mother could continue her translation work for the Dutch Resistance.

One day her courier did not show up. Desperate to continue her work, Mother asked me to take the courier's place. I went to the Central Station every day to deliver my package and pick up a new one. This arrangement worked for quite a while, until 1944. The Allies had been victorious in Belgium and, anticipating that they would take all of the Netherlands, most of the NSB leadership fled to Germany. I was in the station hall with a group of people, and we mocked them as they boarded the trains, those hated Nazi sympathizers. It was a stupid mistake. The Green Police were watching me and I was arrested. One of my friends saw me discreetly drop my package with the incriminating evidence. He rushed to tell my mother what had happened and she immediately disappeared to a safe house. I was loaded in a cattle car with five wounded Canadian soldiers, and we were all deported. Destination: Buchenwald.

In Buchenwald, I was thrust into the worst of all depravities: starvation, heavy labor, terror, exhaustion, and humiliation. Death was everywhere. We were covered in lice, and because the barracks were so crowded, we slept on top of one another along wooden slats. Women were stacked above and below us. Many died from typhus, and I caught it, too. I shriveled to a mere sixty-five pounds, the average weight of a healthy Golden Retriever. On April 11, 1945, the Americans arrived, but it was too late for many. For me, it was just in time; I could not have survived much longer.

The Netherlands had not yet been liberated, so I couldn't go back. I didn't know if my mother was still alive, but I knew my father lived in America. I studied hard to learn English, and soon a fatherly U.S. Army captain took me under his wing. He sent me to a family in the rural area of Northern Germany to be nursed back to health. I was emaciated and gobbled more food than my frail body could handle and, thus, got sick all over again. The family took me to a U.S. Army hospital to recuperate and, later, I got a job as a telephone operator at the American airport in Munich.

When the Netherlands was finally liberated, the Army captain asked the Red Cross to search for my mother and, in 1946, I found her

> About 5 percent of the Dutch were members of the NSB. They were traitors to their own people, and were hated for their affiliation with the Nazis. Not mentioned here are the young Dutch women who fraternized with German soldiers. When the war was over, these women were rounded up and tied to kitchen chairs in front of the school, where their hair was cut and their heads were shaved.

in Utrecht. She was critically ill, another devastating blow to me. In the end, she was admitted to the hospital.

Because the war had interrupted my studies, I had no diplomas, but I desperately wanted to learn. I took the entrance exam for the Art Academy in Amsterdam, where I studied Interior Decorating. Sometime later, my mother was released from the hospital, but she had a relapse and had to go back. This time she had a brain tumor and was in a coma for six months. I couldn't finish my studies because I had to work to provide for us. I found a job at a clockmaker's shop in Amsterdam and worked from 8:00 a.m. to 6:00 p.m. every day. Afterwards, I took the train thirty-five miles back to Utrecht to visit my mother, and then returned to Amsterdam to work until 11:00 p.m. Then I was back on the train to Utrecht to go home to bed!

In 1949, my mother died.

I needed to look forward to my future, not backwards to all that misery, and after a few years, I found a wonderful partner. We married on the Day of the Liberation: May 5, 1950. Together we have made a beautiful life, and I worked as a journalist for a number of art and living magazines, as well as two professional publications. Our son was born in 1953, followed by a daughter in 1954. Our family continued the Montessori tradition, and my children attended the Anne Frank School—formerly called the 6th Montessori School—in Amsterdam.

Even My Baby Sister:
Bram Asscher

My family of five boys attended the 1st Montessori School, and after completing the sixth grade, my oldest brother enrolled in the Jewish high school in 1940, and another brother followed him a year later. When my brother Jaap and I were eight and ten years old, respectively, we had to transfer to the Jewish Montessori School on the Daniel Willinksquare, which was clear on the other side of the city.

The distance was a problem for a couple of reasons. First of all, transportation was an issue. Jews couldn't use the streetcars, so our parents had to find scooters for us to ride to school. Lunchtime was another challenge. Back then, we all went home for lunch, but because we lived so far away it wasn't possible, so we ate with our mother's cousin who lived near the school. Even that didn't last long. In September 1943, all the JEWS ONLY schools were

Left to right: Sallie Asscher, Ies Asscher, a cousin, Jaap Asscher, another cousin and a niece. None of these children survived. (1938)

finally closed down because there were so few Jewish children left. Most had been captured and sent off to concentration camps or had disappeared into hiding.

Our line of boys was finally broken when our baby sister was born in 1943. The *razzias* had intensified, but my parents hoped we could avoid the transport to Westerbork since we had a baby to care for. That was not the case. The horrors of the concentration camp followed, and my youngest brother, who was named Joop, and I were the only ones who survived. The rest of our family died in Bergen-Belsen, just a few weeks before the war was over.

When we were released, Joop and I were sent to live with our cousin, Mickey Lissauer, also a former 1st Montessori School student.

Our aunt and uncle took care of us and made sure we completed our education. I eventually moved to Israel in 1953.

Bram with his wife, Margaliet

Stuffed in a Cattle Car:
Esther Santcroos

I loved my time at the 1st Montessori School. In preschool we learned to button, tie laces, and put the hook through an eye—an old fashioned way of fastening things, but it taught us to dress ourselves. We had our own little rugs to sit on, and we traced big letters cut out of sandpaper. From these letters, we tried to make words, or if we felt like drawing, we could trace large geometric figures. There was also a corner of the room where we could polish real copper or silver. Sometimes we worked in groups and learned how to close a door quietly. If you made too much noise, you had to do it over until you got it right. Years later, I heard a woman close a door, and since it was a bit noisy, she did it again until she got it right. I knew she had gone to a Montessori school!

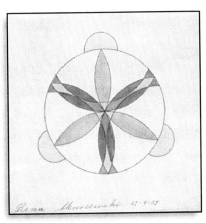

Sample geometric figure the children enjoyed drawing

My brother, Hans—whose name is on the school's Memory Board—was technically inclined. He liked to collect broken alarm clocks, take them apart, and put them back together again. When he was seven or eight, he presented one of his newly "repaired" alarm clocks to me, and I was proud of this gift.

Several disturbing things happened in 1941. To begin with, all Jews had to register with the Census office, so the Germans could track our whereabouts. I was registered as *Erna Santcross,* which is not my real name. My real name is Esther Santcroos, but it seemed safer to register as "Erna" because it sounded less Jewish. Some time before, a family member in England had misspelled our last name as Santcross, rather than Santcroos. When I was registered with the Census office, my parents remembered that incident and recorded the misspelled last name, as a further measure of protection. Although I was quite happy about it at the time, after the war I reverted to my true family name, Santcroos.

That year, the Nazi restrictions on the Jews escalated. In September, Hans and I were sent to the Jewish School on the Jan van Eijckstraat. The Jewish Council had its office right downstairs. We went to the new school for a while, but it wasn't long before all the Jewish schools were shut down. The Nazis used a nearby academic high school as a prison, and when our school was closed, they took all the students and held us captive in that facility. Finally, they marched us across the street to the National Theatre, herded us inside, and locked the doors until we could be shipped off to the concentration camps.

Hans and I sat in the theatre near the exit. At the time, we thought our mother was in the hospital, and we wondered if she would ever know what had happened to us. But before the guards could realize anything was out of order or we knew what was happening, our mother crept in and rescued us. She took us home, and we all went into hiding. Imagine hiding in your own home! Mother was a smart woman, and when she was certain that we, too, would be arrested, she had rented out the rooms in our house. Because people were living there, it hadn't been burglarized like so many of the Jewish homes were. We hid for a while, but eventually someone betrayed us and we were finally arrested.

At first we went to the camp at Westerbork, then we were transported to another camp, Bergen-Belsen, in Northwest Germany, but even that was not our final destination. On April 10, 1945, the Nazis stuffed two thousand of us into cattle cars for the long, grueling ride to another camp—Theresienstadt—where a brand new gas chamber awaited our arrival. We were crammed like sardines on that train for thirteen days, standing for hours at a time with little to no food or water. After nearly two weeks, we ended up in Tröbitz, a village outside Leipzig, Germany, where our train was intercepted by the Russian army. They threw the doors open, coaxed us out, and liberated us from certain death.

It had all been too much for my mother and on May 3, she gave into her exhaustion and died. Hans and I were taken to yet another refugee camp in Riesa, Germany, where he died on May 23. The war was over, and after much wandering around Europe, I eventually made it back to Amsterdam and settled at my aunt's house.

Years later, while I was doing some research in the city archives, I ran across an entry that said we had "left the house without paying the rent." According to the records, my family still owed back rent on the home where we lived when we were arrested.

From the Mouth of Hell:
Jet Edersheim

I started at the 1st Montessori School in January 1940. Like the other girls, I loved going to school where I learned to tie laces and hook shoes, to trace letters and make words, but everything changed the following September when I was transferred to the Jewish School on the Jan van Eijckstraat. The classrooms were full to overflowing, and there were forty-two students in my third grade class, that is, until 1942. The *razzias*

Dossin Barracks in
Mechelen, Belgium

were underway and, slowly but surely, my friends started to disappear, one by one, until our classroom was nearly empty. Because we were Jewish, we lived in constant fear, certain we would be next. In the summer of 1943, my family fled across the border to Belgium and took refuge in a hotel in Tervuren, where we stayed for three months. Then we moved to a small town east of Brussels, and I was enrolled in the Decroly School where I learned to speak French. Despite all our efforts, we could not escape the Nazis, and in 1944, my whole family was arrested and taken to the Belgian transit camp in Dossin. Our next stop was Auschwitz.

We tried everything to keep from being sent to this death camp and, at first, a friend of my father's was able to intervene, and he kept us off the first train. But when the next transport came, we were forced to board. Miraculously, that train never left the station because the Allies marched into Brussels and liberated the city on September 4, 1944. The war in Belgium was finally over, and we had been saved from the mouth of hell. After the Liberation, the nuns from a nearby convent brought over a meal of ham and peas and fed all the prisoners. We were starving and devoured the food, grateful for their kindness.

The Nazis still occupied the Netherlands, so I went back to the Decroly School in Belgium until we went home in May 1945. I finished my elementary education, then studied further at the Montessori Lyceum. Montessori schooling was important to me, and years later I sent my own children to where it all began, the 1st Montessori School in Amsterdam.

A Bullet Through My Knee:
Anny Morpurgo

When we moved to the Old South neighborhood in April 1937, I started preschool at the 1st Montessori School. I remember the long hallways and huge classrooms, and I especially remember Mrs. van Rooy, the head of the preschool. She made me feel welcome. She put me on her lap right away and spoke softly to me in her delicate soprano voice.

I did not, however, like the other kids when I entered elementary school. They argued and pestered each other, and the other girls made harsh comments about my clothes, like you hear about kids doing today. They criticized each other and checked for designer labels. Of course, the atmosphere in any classroom is influenced by the teacher, so perhaps the students weren't the only ones to blame for the unfriendly climate.

Mrs. Joosten-Chotzen,
Dutch Montessori
pioneer

Like so many others, I had to leave 1st Montessori in 1941, because I was Jewish. I transferred to the Jewish Montessori School run by Mrs. Joosten-Chotzen, a friend of Maria Montessori's who had been personally trained by her. Mrs. Joosten-Chotzen was the primary authority on the Montessori movement in the Netherlands, and I was fortunate to attend her school for that year. I clearly remember the day an inspector came to our school and said, "Children, learn as much as you can because nobody can ever take that from you." In retrospect, he must have known the loss we were about to suffer.

It was wartime, and life was dangerous. One morning, I was playing in the square in front of our school and was accidentally shot by an aberrant bullet from an American airplane. The wayward bullet struck me in the knee, and they had to operate to repair the damage. While I was recuperating at home, there was a *razzia* on our street. An officer stormed into our house, took one look at my mother and said, "You are not allowed to work for Jews." He obviously did not think she was Jewish and mistook her for the household help. Even so, our greatest fear was realized: my family was deported to the camp at Westerbork. We stayed at Westerbork for some time, and then the Nazis crammed us on a train bound for Theresienstadt, about thirty-seven miles north of Prague. They put us in the barracks, where we shared a room with twenty to thirty other people. The winter of 1944-45 was desperately cold. The temperature dropped to -25 degrees and, of course, we had no heat and wore only the thin prison clothing we'd been issued. We huddled together to try to keep warm, and even slept one on top of the other, but we were literally freezing to death.

At Theresienstadt, they worked us hard. My father had been given a special status for privileged Jews, so he was able to work in a villa as a handyman and he was also the barber. They put my mother to work in a war materials factory that manufactured the very weapons the Nazis used against us. Because I was very young, I worked in the garden, a job that not only provided some food for us, but sometimes children under ten received extra rations beyond that. Eventually those provisions dwindled, and we all received less...and less...and less... then practically nothing.

When we were liberated by the Russian soldiers, our suffering did not end. Rather than provide relief, the Russians introduced us to their own brand of terror. They behaved like animals. They drank and danced like wild men, then fired their guns at random, simply for their own amusement. In a drunken stupor, they would drag the girls from the orphanage into the woods and have their way with them. Strangely, I was not afraid. I was determined to survive.

Not only had we nearly frozen to death, we almost starved to death, too. After the Liberation, my girlfriend and I begged for food, and we managed to get a little. Then, in July 1945, we were taken to Dobrjani, a refugee camp run by the Americans. The Americans obviously did not understand how much we had suffered under the Nazis because they allowed their German prisoners to keep an eye on us, a particularly vile offense.

In early August, the Americans took us back to the Netherlands, and that trip was yet another terrifying experience. The small, open airplane seated about ten people, and we flew straight into a violent thunderstorm with absolutely no protection from the rain, the wind, or the lightning. It was a hell of another kind.

Despite the storm, we arrived safely at the Philips factory in Eindhoven where other large groups of people had been transported. These many years later, I can still close my eyes and see those bunk beds stacked high. We were only there for a few days before we found a truck to take us home to Amsterdam.

Our troubles were far from over, but we were on our way home. When we got to Amsterdam, we had to register in order to get ration cards to buy food. Nearly everything was rationed; there was so little to go around. Our country had been devastated, and it took a long time to recover. We moved to the center of the city where my father started a business from home. I was still a girl and started classes at the HBS, my academic high school.

The Netherlands eventually healed, but I did not. I have never fully recovered, even though many decades have passed. My experience in the concentration camps has caused me to withdraw from others, to be continually cautious and suspicious. Deep inside, I still feel unwanted— the feeling of being an outcast never leaves me.

Begging for Food:
Cora Landzaat

My sister and I joined the 1st Montessori School as preschoolers in the late 1930s. The Montessori teaching materials were made for me. I loved to play with all the educational toys and the cabinets were full of them. The best part was that I could help myself to whatever I wanted. It was a lovely, carefree time.

My best girlfriends were Lieke Roos and Colette La Croix. I also remember Eric Vriesinga, a good-looking boy whom I liked very much! In 1941, my Jewish friends had to leave our school, including my best friend Lieke. I missed her terribly.

My parents had a mixed marriage, and although my mother was Jewish, my sister and I were allowed to stay at our school because our father was not. Before 1943, marriages between Jews and non-Jews were frowned upon, but not yet targeted by the Nazis. But the Germans were not the only ones who disapproved of such a match. Years earlier, when my father told his parents he was marrying a Jewish girl, his own father became so angry that he knocked him down the stairs! My parents eventually married, and my Jewish grandparents—whom I loved very much—lived with us. I actually liked them best!

In 1942, the *razzias* began. When they came to our street, the Nazis arrested my grandparents because a five-year-old neighbor boy told them, "There are Jews living in that house over there." My mother had worn the yellow Jewish star since that May, but at some point she had taken it off and dyed her hair to disguise herself. Since they didn't recognize her as a Jew, she was not taken.

Like many of the Dutch, we did what we could to oppose the Germans. My father was a member of an important Dutch Resistance group that included Willem Schermerhorn, who later became the first post-war prime minister. To assist them, my mother, sister, and I spent hours tearing their important notes and papers into tiny pieces before we flushed them down the toilet. Eventually my father got caught and was transported to a prison camp in the province of Groningen. Many of the Dutch Resistance workers were either executed or sent to concentration camps but, quite miraculously, my father was released from prison and came home.

In the spring of 1944, my sister and I had a little altercation of our own. When we were walking home from school, two of the older boys shoved us into a doorway and tried to kiss us! My parents were furious and met with the principal, Mr. Eijgenstein, who made sure it never happened again.

In September 1944, I was ready to start sixth grade, but because Mother was Jewish, living in Amsterdam had become too dangerous for our family, so we went into hiding. We took a train to Ede, a city in the center of the Netherlands. The trip was awful because I was so afraid—afraid of the conductor, afraid there would be a German inspection, afraid of everything. We knew the Allied forces regularly bombed the railway tracks, so we were afraid of that, too.

"If a German asks you anything," my father warned, "act like you don't understand him. Just pretend you're not there!" My little body rebelled against these extreme fears, and I remember how bloated I was from the stress. Fortunately, all went well and we arrived in Ede in one piece, where we stayed in a private school for boys near a factory complex.

Several days later, on Sunday, September 17, the sirens sounded that warned us of approaching aircraft. We ran outside to the ditches that had been dug as bomb shelters and jumped in with twenty-six other people. When the factory and a nearby mansion were hit, we all ended up in a jumbled heap in the ditch. It was pitch black. I heard my mother call out for my father, who turned out to be smack on top of her!

After the bombing, there were dead bodies everywhere. I was

horrified. We obviously had to leave that place, so our group started walking towards Arnhem. We stopped at a farmhouse and stayed there for several days, spending much of our time cowering under heavy tables while the bombing continued. Some Germans arrived and ordered us to leave, so we started walking again, hoping to get to the nearby village of Lunteren. We traveled through the forest because we thought it would be safer, but the Germans drove through the trails like maniacs, firing at anything that moved, including us. In order to stay alive I had to run as fast as I could, then throw myself flat on the ground and lie perfectly still, then get up and run again. I was certain I would die at any moment.

Eventually we reached Lunteren and found a summer cottage in the woods where we could stay. It had an enclosed porch where all our men hid. A few days later, a group of Nazi soldiers came by, and demanded to know if we had any men in the house. I guess our group thought I had a big mouth, so they shoved me out front to answer them, even though I was only twelve years old. I pretended to understand the Germans and managed to answer "no, no, no" to all their questions. We were terrified, but the Nazis must have believed me because they went away.

During the winter of 1944, food was very scarce and the cold was extreme. We traveled from farm to farm, riding bicycles without tires and begging for food. When the snow started to fall, we traveled on a sled. My mother always made me ask for the food because I was small and pale and pathetic. She hoped they would take pity on me. We never got much, only beets—sugar beets—morning, noon, and night! Sometimes we experimented and tried to make an omelet, or soup, or a puree. Most of the time we were sick; we were weak and had little resistance left. For months we were all crammed together in that small place. Five children slept on two mattresses in one room. On more than a few occasions, tempers flared.

There was not much for us to do, but outside my father dug a deep pit for our family, in case there was another air raid. He even created places for us to sit, and the pit was so deep that when I sat down I couldn't see a speck of the sky. We couldn't get out of the pit without help!

In April 1945, when it became clear that the war would end soon, the SS ordered us to evacuate the house. Although the war was over, transportation in the Netherlands was difficult. We rode in horse-drawn carts and waved white flags for protection, traveling west towards Amersfoort. We went about eighteen miles until we reached a school where we slept on the floor for two days. From there, we continued to Hilversum where a family took us in and gave us one of their rooms. We stayed there until the Liberation on May 5, 1945.

When we finally got back to Amsterdam, we found out that while we were gone, a pediatrician had seized our home, sold everything of value, and burned everything made of wood. The house was stripped bare; we had absolutely nothing. By that time, my sister and I were too old to return to the 1st Montessori School. Eventually our family moved to a village south of Amsterdam, and we joined the HBS, the five-year academic high school. But we were too far behind in our studies and the school was too difficult for us, so we were transferred to two separate high schools. Neither of us liked our school, but we managed to finish our education.

Life was impossible for my father after the war. He had been very fond of my grandparents who were murdered in Auschwitz, and many of his friends had been executed or had not returned from the camps. For a while he worked for a broadcasting company, but after such a long period of extreme tension and stress, he developed a brain tumor and died at age 65.

We survived the war, but the war has never left me. At times, my grief from the loss of so many friends and family members was unbearable. To come to grips with that, a friend and I later spent several days in Auschwitz, which was a critical step in my healing.

Sent Off to Strangers:
Roos Groenman

Ever since I was a young girl, my parents told my brother, sister, and me that, although the Netherlands was a very good country, one day we would all go to Israel to help build the Jewish land. My parents were Zionists and felt that, as Jews, our true home was in Israel. Before the war started, we heard rumors that the Nazis were abusing the Jews in Germany. In fact, in 1938, a young German came to the Netherlands and gathered a group of young Jews together to warn them about what was happening in Germany. His advice was to pack up everything and flee to Israel before it was too late. Most of the Jews could not manage that—their parents were too old, they had their work, and how could they leave everything behind? So they continued with their lives until the war broke out.

On February 7, 1940, I started at the 1st Montessori preschool and continued there until second grade, when I had to move to a JEWS ONLY school. I don't remember much about those years, but I do remember wearing that awful yellow star on my clothes at all times.

As things got worse, my parents were determined to keep their children safe, no matter what they had to do. They found an organization that placed Jewish children in hiding, and soon the three of us were saying goodbye to our entire family—our grandmother, uncle, aunt, cousins, and our parents—who all lived together. I had no idea that my family would soon be arrested and deported to Bergen-Belsen.

> When Jewish parents realized they could not escape their own tragic end, they enlisted the help of the Dutch Resistance or Christian organizations to keep their children safe. Such groups hid the children and found foster families to raise them until their parents returned.

We were sent to a farm near the Belgian border, and my brother's name was immediately changed to conceal his Jewish identity. His real name was Sal, but we now had to call him "Sjef," which was hard for me to remember. I often forgot his new name, and one time I called him Sal by mistake. One of the other girls asked who I was talking to and, thinking quickly, I told her I was remembering a friend who sat next to me in my old school.

The other children were from rural areas and enjoyed the farm, but we missed our city life. We wanted to use a toilet, rather than a hole in the ground. We missed our comfortable beds and had to sleep on a haystack. The others were giddy when a rabbit or pig was slaughtered and made a game of it, but we were horrified. They would grab one of the butchered limbs and chase after us city kids—a fun game for them, but for us it was miserable.

Fortunately, we were only there for several weeks before we were moved again. We had serious infections all over our arms and legs and, for a while, we stayed with a kind woman who tended us until our wounds healed. After that, we were taken to the city of Haarlem where they split us up; we were each sent to a separate family. The family I joined already had five children. It did not take the Germans long to find out that I was not registered, so I was immediately whisked away to a small village in the eastern part of the Netherlands. After that, I was moved every two weeks.

My eleventh home was in Warmond, where I lived for over a year. The adults were kind to me, and I stayed in contact with them for a very long time after the war. Two other children lived there, but at the time, I didn't know they were Jews in hiding, too.

Although we lived out in the country, the signs of war were all around us. Our large farmhouse was in the middle of a field, not far from a train and car viaduct that was frequently a target for bombings. The German army was garrisoned nearby, between our farm and Warmond, and every day I had to ride my bicycle past them to get to school. I was terrified I would be caught. One day, I was a little late coming home and it was getting dark. One of the soldiers raised his gun, aimed straight at me, and pretended to shoot. I was certain I was going to die; I have never forgotten that dreadful feeling.

Miraculously, our parents returned from Bergen-Belsen and they located all three of us. We went back to Amsterdam, and I remember going somewhere and staying in a huge room with countless other people, but to this day, I have no idea what that was. When we found our own place to live, we tried to become a family again. My siblings and I went back to school and to the Jewish Youth Organization. I assumed we would be going to Israel at some point, especially since my brother Sal and some others began preparations to start a kibbutz, a rural community where all possessions and responsibilities are shared. Unfortunately, my parents' marriage didn't last, and they divorced. My father stayed in the Netherlands, and my mother, sister, and I moved to Israel where my mother lived until she died. My brother emigrated to Israel later, and he lived in the kibbutz he started with some friends.

Shuffled Around the Netherlands:
Sal Groenman

I honestly don't remember the time I spent at the 1st Montessori School because it was so short. My family had moved from Haarlem to Amsterdam in February 1940—when I was seven years old—and in the fall of 1941, we had to move to a JEWS ONLY school. The tension at my new school was unbearable. Every day, both the students and teachers vanished—captured in the *razzias* and deported to who knows where. You never knew who would be next and feared it would be you.

> The Merchant Marines were sailors who operated cargo ships and shipped goods throughout the world. Each ship had a captain, a first mate, a second mate, a navigator, and many sailors. When the Nazis invaded, the cargo ships that were out to sea dared not return because the Germans would have arrested them, confiscated their goods, and taken over their ships for the German war effort. The Germans built no ships of their own.
>
> The Merchant Marines had to change course, get their ships to England, and join the Allies to share their knowledge of the waters and the shipping routes with them. Sailing home would have been disastrous for them and the Netherlands.

In September 1942, I was ten years old, and because my parents were convinced that our family would soon be deported, they sent my sisters and me away to safety. At first we stayed at a large farm near Belgium and my parents received regular reports about our well-being, but the communications soon stopped; my parents had been rounded up in a *razzia*.

When we left the farm, we were sent to Haarlem to a friend's house from our former preschool, but we couldn't stay long; we used to live in that neighborhood and the people knew who we were. That's when my sisters and I were separated. I was placed with a Merchant Marine family on the other side of the city whose father, an officer with the Marines, had been at sea when the Nazis invaded and could not return to the Netherlands.

After that, another single mother with three sons took me in, and I attended a nearby Christian school, where I was registered under my new name, Sjef. The "hunger winter" of 1944 to 1945 was intolerable. The temperatures plunged and we had no heat, no fuel for cooking, and barely anything to eat. I stayed with this family until February 1945, and when they could no longer care for me, I was placed in the Institute for Seaman's Children. At the Institute, we lived in a large shed where tables, beds, and chairs had been placed to create scant living quarters, but it was cold and stark, and we were famished.

The rest of the world must have known we were hungry because the week before the Liberation, they came to our rescue. I watched as parcels of food, including Swedish white bread, were thrown from American bombers to the starving population below. They intervened just in time; many of us were near death.

After we were liberated, I went back to my preschool friend's house and stayed with them until June 30, 1945. That day, my parents came home from Bergen-Belsen and our family was reunited. Our house had been seized by the Nazis, so we stayed in a refugee center in Amsterdam for a while. In 1951, my mother and sisters moved to Israel, but I went to the Center for Israel Pioneers and emigrated to Israel later that year with several other young people. I wanted to help build the Jewish state and felt I'd been groomed to do so for years. Our Zionist tradition, our education at home, and the effects of the Second World War all contributed to my passion for Israel, and I was determined to do my part. Our family name of Groenman was eventually changed to "Golan" because the people in Israel could not pronounce our Dutch name. And why did we choose the name Golan? Because our kibbutz was in Amiad across the Golan Heights!

The Ones Left Behind

My Parents Imprisoned:
Floris Haak

I wasn't the first boy in our family to go to the 1st Montessori School. When I joined the preschool in September 1936, my brother Bob was in the fifth grade, and my oldest brother and two sisters attended the Montessori Lyceum. Five years later the war started, and our family immediately joined the Dutch Resistance. My mother processed ration cards, and through the efforts of my sister Tineke, we hid Jewish people in our home for a day or two until more permanent lodging could be found for them. We eventually housed two Jewish girls ourselves.

As the war progressed, the Nazis arrested thousands of Jewish students and held them at the National Theatre until they could be deported to the transit camp at Westerbork. My sister Tineke rescued many of these children and brought them to our home. She and her friends saved many little children and ultimately found hiding places for them in Friesland and Limburg.

Hiding Jews was not only dangerous, it was expensive. We had to raise money to buy food ration cards for them, and they needed some cash, too. My father taught mathematics at both the Montessori Lyceum and the Amsterdam Lyceum, and he worked evenings as well. To supplement his earnings, we sold copies of the poem "Song of the Eighteen Dead," written by Jan Campert, who had been arrested for helping the Jews. This famous poem described the Nazi execution of eighteen Dutch Resistance fighters. The poem was forbidden, and we had boxes full of it.

It was the summer of 1943, and I was about to enter the Montessori Lyceum. On August 3, my brother Bob delivered a box of the poems to the Boissevain family, who were members of a militant Dutch Resistance group that specialized in weapons and liquidations. When he rang their doorbell, the maid answered, but delivered him straight into the hands of the SD, who were arresting everyone who went to that house. Bob was taken to prison, and the SD immediately came to see us.

It so happened that my mother had just received a stack of ration cards from the Dutch Resistance, and she was still at the front door. I was already in my pajamas and ready to go to bed. My grown sister, Mieke, had come from a nearby village to visit us on her day off, and she was still there. The SD arrested both my parents and took them to prison, but they didn't arrest Mieke. My parents convinced the officers that she had simply stopped by and was not part of our household. Thankfully, the two Jewish girls we were hiding were not discovered!

The next morning, Mieke took the girls to a new safe house, and I went home with her for about two weeks. As soon as she was able to quit her job, we returned to Amsterdam together so that I could start school at the Montessori Lyceum. Eventually my brother Bob was released, and he was able to prepare for his final exams and graduate.

We missed our parents, and the only official contact we had with them was when we went to the prison to pick up their dirty laundry. They were housed in separate buildings, and I knew the precise location of each of their cells. I wanted them to know what was happening in our family, so I went down one street and shouted out our news to my father, then went down the other to repeat it to my mother. They needed to know that Tineke was still free and was working hard for the Dutch Resistance.

That communication worked for a time, but we really wanted to see them face-to-face. Mieke managed to get permission for us to visit them at the prison on October 7, 1943—their twenty-fifth wedding anniversary. When we arrived, we found out they had been moved to Vught, a concentration camp in the southern part of the Netherlands. Political prisoners were often sent to Vught to work in factories where they built weapons for the Nazis to use against the Allied forces, the very armies we prayed would rescue us from the German occupation. The prisoners often sabotaged the machinery so that the ammunition they produced would be defective and couldn't be used against us.

Although we were devastated they had been moved, it was an improvement for them. When they were loaded on the streetcar for transport, my parents looked out and, to their great joy, they saw me walking to school. It was the last time my parents ever saw me; to this day, I wish I had seen them, too. We thought they were only going away for six months or so. We didn't know they had been sentenced to prison until the end of the war.

In Vught, my mother and father both worked for the Philips Commando. The Philips Company was one of the largest private companies in the Netherlands that had been taken over by the Nazis. The plant was run by Frits Philips, who hand-selected the prisoners to work in his facility. These prisoners were fortunate; they were given a hot meal every day. My father worked in the mathematics lab and my mother was in the tool factory. Though they were assigned to separate areas, they got to see one another regularly and even managed to talk now and then.

The prisoners were only allowed to receive one letter per week. Tineke wrote to them, disguising herself as "cousin Erni" because her work for the Dutch Resistance was way too dangerous for her to be identified as their daughter. In addition to her short letters, sometimes we even managed to send them a little food.

In May 1944, my parents were separated forever. Many of the men, including my father, were transferred to Dachau, the concentration camp in Germany. He was later sent to Sachsenhausen, another infamous camp, where he died in January 1945.

On September 5, 1944, all the prisoners who were still in Vught were herded into cattle cars and taken to Germany. The women, about 600 of them, were sent to the women's concentration

The transport from Vught to Ravensbruck was documented in detail in the book *The Hiding Place*, the biography of another Dutch Resistance worker, Corrie ten Boom.

camp at Ravensbruck, including my mother and two friends she had made in Vught. Because they claimed they had experience working with radio tubes, they all got a special assignment and were moved to Reichenbach, where they worked in an electronics factory as specialists in radio techniques. Just a few months later my mother caught malaria, and she died on December 6, 1944.

Losing both my parents by such cruel means has been hard for me, but I have always been very proud of both of them and the work they did for the Netherlands during the Nazi occupation. That knowledge, coupled with my memories of them, has consoled me for all these years.

Saving Jewish Children:
Elly de Zwart

I walked into my preschool class on August 25, 1937, and was a student at the 1st Montessori School all the way through the sixth grade. I remember that starting third grade was an exciting time when we would finally be promoted from the younger classes. The new rooms were upstairs, and we would be mingling with the upper grades, a promotion I eagerly anticipated. For years we had all looked forward to that day, but when my turn came things didn't go as planned. In September 1941, the Jewish students had to move to JEWS ONLY schools and, because of that, our Jewish sixth graders couldn't advance to the HBS or Lyceum with their other classmates. They had to stay put until their school was ready, even though they had already graduated. Until they left, there was no room for us upstairs.

Then all the Jewish students were transferred, and my classroom seemed empty. When we finally got to move upstairs, instead of being happy, I remember the awful emptiness I felt because all my little friends were gone. The joy of moving upstairs, of advancing with my classmates, had vanished.

Our family was active in the Dutch Resistance, and my parents helped shelter Jewish children who were in hiding, either because their own parents had been captured and deported to concentration camps or because their parents had voluntarily sent them away to keep them safe. We placed those children with surrogate parents who took care of them until the war ended, and I helped out a number of times. When I got home from school, I would play with whatever child was there, usually a three- or four-year-old. Then my father would give me an address, and I got on my scooter and delivered the child to the next safe house. I did this a number of times when I was only ten years old.

In 1944, I graduated from the elementary school and started at the Montessori Lyceum. We wore wooden shoes back then, and at lunchtime I clattered over to the soup kitchen to eat with my friends. The Netherlands suffered from a severe lack of food during the war, and since we were children, we were allowed to eat at the soup kitchen. On occasion, I even managed to sneak some food out for my parents.

My early days as a Montessori child made an indelible impression on me, and because I loved that learning environment, I studied to become a teacher and earned my Montessori training credentials. For forty years I taught at the 6th Montessori School—now called the Anne Frank School—and enjoyed a fulfilling career.

Bad Boy:
Fred Huijser

I started kindergarten at the 3rd Montessori school, but after three years, they kicked me out! The principal decided that, because of my frequent mischief and bad behavior, I would be transferred to the 1st Montessori School, if I could get permission from their principal, Miss Strengers. Who knows why she agreed to admit me? In August 1938, I was nearly eight years old and in the second grade—and still acting up. I remember our teacher would sometimes punish the boys by making us wear aprons, which was quite humiliating to me. Whenever our class got too loud, Miss Strengers would walk in unexpectedly and an eerie silence would fall over us; it was as if the Holy Mary herself had appeared and we were struck silent before her.

Since my new school was not near my home, getting to school was difficult. I usually walked to and from school, but my parents gave my teacher extra streetcar tickets to use in case it rained. On those days, I'd board the tram a block from school and ride to my house near the Hercules Street stop. My parents closely monitored my trip home, and my teacher cooperated by recording the exact time I left school.

As I said, I was a handful, and I continued to act up at the 1st Montessori School. In the winter, I put rubber bands on the hot classroom stove, and they stank up the entire floor when they melted. When I used the restroom, I often "aimed" wrong on purpose, and they had to appoint someone to monitor my bathroom breaks. Like most young students, we wrote and passed notes to each other in class, and at one point, the teacher took the box where I'd saved all my notes and burned it in the stove that heated our classroom!

My teacher also taught French, but in 1941, the Nazis forbade schools from teaching the language, so she moved the lessons to her house. I went there one day per week. I had never been in a teacher's home before and didn't expect to meet her husband. He was an unemployed architect who was so short that one day she teased, "When we go on vacation, I put him in my suitcase!"

In the fifth and sixth grades I had a new teacher, Miss Heymeijer, and I learned a lot from her. She taught both language and math, and I remember feeling grateful for what I had learned from her throughout my high school years. Our math books were very difficult, with math problems that even the teachers today don't know how to tackle! Our text contained 400 such problems, and I loved them! Here's an example:

> A and B leave at the same time from P to R.
> A leaves at 9:00; arrives at R 11:15.
> B leaves at 9:15; arrives at R 10:55.
> What is the distance if A travels 28 meters less per minute than B?

I was still not particularly well behaved, but I had learned to control myself a little better by that time. On occasion, Miss Heymeijer had to step in when I got out of hand, and she would write a letter I had to take home that said something like, "Freddy again managed to idle away his time. Please sign and return." I never showed those notes to my parents. Instead I took a piece of my father's stationary, wrote out a response, and then signed his name. Unfortunately, Miss Heymeijer was not fooled!

When the war started, air raid sirens often interrupted classes. Everyone had to march downstairs to the kindergarten section, singing "one-two-one-two," and we stayed there until the all-clear signal was sounded. Sometimes I got to ring the bell that signaled students to return to their classrooms. Ringing the bell was a privilege that I, of course, abused at times!

In December 1941, Mr. Eijgenstein became our new principal. He was a person of strong authority, and one day I was late to class and had to bring a note from my parents the next day. Again, I stole my father's stationery and forged an excuse. When Mr. Eijgenstein walked in my classroom later that morning, I cringed, thinking I'd been caught, but he was there to discuss a different matter with my teacher. Mr. Eijgenstein was also our history teacher, and during his lessons, he often demonstrated historical moments by acting out the parts of famous men. I specifically remember when he portrayed Napoleon's flight to Elba and shouted out, "Here I am, shoot me if that's what you want!"

Our school was also used for other purposes during the war. On May 13, 1943, everyone had to turn their radios over to the Germans, and they were collected in the 1st Montessori School gym under strict Nazi control. Each person was given a receipt for what they turned in. My father was clever. He handed over a brand new radio that had been stripped of its insides and fitted with the guts from an old radio. The new radio was hidden at home in a palm plant, and we continued to use it whenever we thought it was safe to listen. It was risky; anyone caught listening to the BBC risked being sent to a concentration camp, and some were even shot for the offense. We continued to tune in until the fall of 1944, but after that there was no more electricity, so we got all our war news from illegal Underground newsletters.

Nazi Youth Member:
Jan Ponne

I started at the 1st Montessori School on October 1, 1934, when I was a four-year-old boy. My parents had already joined the NSB, a political party comparable to the Nazi party in Germany, although members of the Dutch NSB were often critical of Hitler. Just as all children are influenced by their parents' politics, I was influenced by mine. I was a child; I simply followed their lead.

On May 10, 1940, the Germans invaded the Netherlands which, to our family, was not unhappy news. My tenth birthday was a few days later, and I wanted to canvass the neighborhood to congratulate our neighbors on this turn of events. My mother, however, warned me not to do that. I clearly had no understanding of what war meant, had no idea about what was to come, and did not realize that to most of the Dutch, the invasion was the kiss of death.

Because of their own political affiliation, my parents expected me to become a member of the NSB Youth Group, a close parallel to the Hitler Youth in Germany. I was happy to do so, and proudly wore my uniform to school one Saturday, the day of our weekly NSB Youth meetings. After that, my classmates turned against me. Whenever our teacher left the room or when we were out at recess, they ridiculed me. They laughed at me and taunted me, merciless in their mocking. I thought I was strong enough to handle their disdain until the entire class conspired together to declare me non-existent. They would completely ignore me, and then knock into me as if I was invisible, although I was clearly their target. My mother complained on my behalf and our teacher put a stop to it, but

> Children in the Netherlands went to school Monday through Saturday, but were released at noon on both Wednesdays and Saturdays and could pursue their other interests.

I was still an outcast, and it hurt.

The Youth Group meetings took place in the center of the city, usually on Saturday afternoons. The ten- to thirteen-year-olds were called Seagulls, and once we got older we could join the Stormers. We learned how to march, we sang songs about the Fatherland, and we practiced knotting ropes. The inspections were strict, and our uniforms—light-blue blouses with seagull insignias, shoulder pads, and a ties around the neck—had to be perfect.

I soon learned that the unquestioned obedience to military orders did not suit my personality, so I told my parents I wanted to quit. Now we had a problem: How does one quit a Nazi group? My brother Henk came up with a brilliant solution. He knew that the Music Corps was far less militaristic and that they needed someone to play the trumpet. Because I loved music and had been taking piano lessons for ten years, I was intrigued by the idea. I started taking lessons from a trumpet player from the National Concert Hall and, in short order, he taught me how to play. So instead of attending those Saturday meetings, I went to the Music Corps practices, and every now and then our band played in a parade or some other event.

Back at school, the results of the Nazi occupation were unfolding. I clearly remember when my classmate Leo had to tell me good-bye because all the Jewish children had to go to a JEWS ONLY school. I was very sad about that because he was such a nice friend. I knew I could speak freely about this at home since my parents strongly opposed the separation of the Jews, although they considered the rumors about annihilation camps to be Allied propaganda. It was only after the war, when documentary films exposed the horror of those camps, that my parents finally accepted the ugly truth—that many Jews had, indeed, been exterminated.

In the summer of 1942, I started at the HBS and the first two years went fairly smoothly. But at the beginning of my junior year, on September 5, 1944—Dolle Dinsdag—we heard that the Allied Forces were advancing in the south. This news created a panic for those of us who were in the NSB, because, as Nazi supporters, we would be the targets of their assault. My father was a police officer in charge of the Black Market. He was told he was being transferred to Germany and that our family should immediately board the train for Berlin. My mother and I went to the Central station in Amsterdam and located the assigned train. It was already packed with others who were fleeing the country.

We managed to squeeze aboard, but it was a dangerous trip. The Allied troops were effective. They derailed the trains and sabotaged the tracks. Whenever a train was attacked, all the passengers had to get off to seek shelter, but there wasn't anywhere to go. We were lucky; our train got as far as the small station near Bremen, Germany. We never did make it to Berlin, and we later learned that my father wasn't sent to Germany after all.

Dolle Dinsdag (Crazy Tuesday), September 5, 1944, was the day that the Allied Forces had made such progress after the Normandy landings that the occupied countries expected immediate liberation. This, however, did not happen.

In Bremen, they took us to a local school gym where we stayed for a few days. One of the ladies there took a liking to my mother and made arrangements for us to move into an apartment on the first floor of her building. We had to work to earn our keep; my mother was assigned to the kitchen, and I worked in a furniture factory with a Russian girl and another boy from the Netherlands.

In January 1945, my brother Henk showed up unannounced. He was working for the Nazis as a chauffeur, and he drove us back across the border to the Netherlands. From there, we took the train as far as Assen and stayed there for a time until we could continue on to Amsterdam. In Assen, I worked in a bookstore that had gone out of business, sorting the valuable books that were to be saved from the worthless ones. Eventually my father came by car to take us back to Amsterdam.

On May 7, 1945, just two days after the Liberation, the Canadians took full control of the city, and my father was arrested at his office.

Mother was arrested at home. We were all Nazi sympathizers, but because I was a boy, they left me behind and told me to report to another agency. I had no intention of reporting to anyone—anywhere—and although I didn't follow the orders, I knew I had to leave our house. I drifted through the city for a while, staying here and there until I ran into a friend who took me home with him. It took some convincing, but his mother allowed me to stay with them, but not for long.

We had relatives who lived about sixty miles away, so I decided to ride my old bike to their home, hoping they would take me in. I barely reached the outskirts of Amsterdam before my wheel gave way, so I had to go back to my friend's house. No one was happy to see me.

In the meantime, it became clear that most of the country's roads and bridges had been blown up in the war, which left only one way to get to the southern part of the country—by boat. I found a boat that was headed south, but that would only get me partway to my destination, so I took a train headed towards the southern province of Zeeland. When I finally reached my relatives' home, they lectured me about how wrong my parents had been to support the Nazis, to turn against their own countrymen, and to aid the enemy. It was hard for me to bear these accusations, but I hung my head and accepted their condemnation; I needed a place to stay. Although they were disappointed in my parents, they lovingly accepted me into their family and I felt very fortunate.

My mother was not in prison for long. She moved in with my grandmother, and in the summer of 1946, we were reunited in Amsterdam. One afternoon the phone rang and I answered it. The voice on the other end told me that my brother Henk had died. He, too, had been imprisoned after the war and had volunteered to be part of a detail that removed leftover land mines from the beaches. His reward for this service was one hot meal

> Between 1945 and 1947, German prisoners and Dutch Nazi sympathizers were used to remove land mines left behind by the Germans. Fifty Dutch and two hundred Germans lost their lives. The effort took many years, and the activity continued until 2007. A total of 1.8 million mines were finally cleared.

every day. When he entered the bunker after finishing his work one night, he stepped on a mine himself and was instantly killed. I listened, then hung up the phone. I knew I had to tell my mother and grandmother, but I wasn't up to the task. It was the most difficult moment of my life, even to this day. When I walked in the room, I was so overcome by stress that I passed out and fell flat on the ground. A couple of days later, Henk's casket was brought to the cemetery, but we never looked at his body. They let my father out of prison for that one day to attend the funeral; he was a man broken by grief and shame.

In 1948, my father was fully released, and shortly thereafter my parents took over a private nursing home for seniors with dementia. My father handled the administration and registration, and my mother presided over the kitchen. We lived on the ground floor, and the patients lived upstairs where they were attended by nurses. Our family fell into a routine again and I often worked in the garden, mingling with the patients.

I continued my studies and got a degree in theology, and in 1960, I met and married my wife. We worked for a number of years for the Dutch Protestant Movement and had three sons. Eventually we moved to Arnhem, where I became the director of the Freethinking Forming Center. I stayed there until the project ran out of funds, but in the meantime, I had been attending seminars about Gestalt psychology, a psychological theory that is famous for its assertion that "the whole is greater than the sum of its parts." There I met an American, Dr. Alexander Lowen, the founder of Biofeedback and Analysis, which is a particular form of psychotherapy based on the mind-body connection. My wife and I were among the first in the country to be trained in this technique. We started our own practice based on biofeedback, and together with my colleague Jan Velzeboer, I started the first Institute for Biofeedback Analysis in the Netherlands.

A German Hiding Jews:
Karin de Jongh

I started at the 1st Montessori School when my family moved to Amsterdam from The Hague in 1935. I was seven years old, and our principal, Miss Strengers, spent much of her time advocating for peace. Every year on November 11, she called the whole school together for an assembly on Armistice Day. On the day the Nazis invaded the Netherlands, the children and teachers had drawn up a petition to support peace, but it was to no avail. We were already at war.

Just eighteen days later, a Nazi officer came to meet with Miss Strengers. He was there for me. I didn't know what I had done or what was happening, but I was told to gather my things, put on my coat, and go outside. They handed me over to a soldier who carried a machine gun, and he took me to the Kaiser Wilhelm Gymnasium where I was immediately tested and placed in the freshman class.

> Under Nazi rule, German citizens in the Netherlands could only send their children to German schools.

I found out that this school was only for children who had German parents. Never mind that our family had fled to the Netherlands to escape the German regime. I never thought of myself as a German—I considered myself a Dutch girl who had a German passport! Apparently, the Nazis were separating the Germans who lived in the Netherlands from the Dutch, and they forbade us to be educated together.

It was a painful transition. I had left the open Montessori environment to be thrust into a narrow, rigid educational system, and I was miserable. They immersed me in all things German. I could only speak German, and I had to listen to the German teachers bark it back at me. Every morning they raised the German flag and I had to sing the German national anthem. Further, I had to click my heels and raise my right arm to make the Hitler greeting. I couldn't have been more unhappy.

The school officials obviously didn't know our secret: After the war broke out, my parents had joined the Dutch Resistance. We hid Jews in our home, and because of that, every day I was flung back and forth from one world into another. I was barely fourteen, but carried a huge burden—at school I was taught that people in the Dutch Resistance were evil, while all along, we had a Jewish family living with us! I had to be extremely careful, had to be very guarded in everything I did or said. I was a teenager, but I could never bring a girlfriend home, nor was I ever invited to do homework with a friend or sleep over at her house. During my teen years I never shared my feelings, laughed myself silly, asked any questions, or made any friends. I was like a frozen statue; those years were hell.

One day, we read the poem "Die Lorelei" in class. At the bottom, it said, "poet unknown." After all the restraint I'd exhibited, I could not help myself. I had to contribute something, had to be heard. Before I knew it, I blurted out that the poet was the well-known Heinrich Heine, a Jew. I immediately knew I shouldn't have done that, and was severely punished for my blunder.

On September 5, 1944, the Nazis feared the Allied forces would invade the Netherlands and take the country back. It was Dolle Dinsdag—Crazy Tuesday, as we call it now—a day of fierce panic. The Germans packed everyone and everything they could into cattle cars to take back to Germany, and they stuffed prisoners in the train cars with no toilet, no fresh air, no room to move or even sit down. The people had nothing to drink and no food. They closed down my school that day, and because I was German, there was no other school for me to attend, no other place for me to go. Sadly, the Allies did not invade that day; they didn't arrive for nine more months. I never went back to school in the Netherlands, but years later, on my fifty-fifth birthday, I was finally awarded my high school diploma.

From Communists to Resistance Workers:
Rudi Leikies

My parents were communists who had come from Germany in 1927. They worked for the Soviets as Russian exporters in the Netherlands, first in Rotterdam and later in Amsterdam. In 1938, the year I was born, they were fired from their Soviet Russian Export jobs because they disagreed with Stalin's politics. They most definitely did not want to move back to Germany under the Hitler regime, so we stayed in Amsterdam where my father took over a wine shop.

When the war started, my parents were active in both the Dutch and the German Resistance. They had many roles; they were the contact for obtaining identity cards, were the staff of a "destruction-execution" group, and they provided a hiding place for Jews on the run.

In 1944, I was a student at the 1st Montessori School, and Mr. Eijgenstein was the principal. He warned my parents that, because children of German citizens were ordered to attend German schools, my parents—not he—would be solely responsibility for my being there. If the Germans inspected the school and discovered my background, the principal would claim he didn't know my parents were German. Although my presence presented a potential danger to the school, Mr. Eijgenstein allowed me to attend under those conditions.

At one point, a number of Resistance fighters were arrested in Berlin and Amsterdam, and one of them fingered the Soviet Russian Export business where my parents used to work as a possible center of activity. My parents were somehow implicated, and we received frequent visits from the SD, including the feared SD officer, Herbert Oelschlagel, who was later assassinated by the Dutch Resistance. To avenge his assassination, the Germans set two villas on the corners of the Apollolane and the Beethovenstraat on fire, then rounded up all the men between the ages of fifteen and fifty who lived on that block and shot them in the street, execution style. I saw the very first flowers that were placed where those twenty-nine men and boys were put to death. Since the execution happened after curfew, it was an amazing testament that someone would risk his or her own life to honor those who died.

Even after Oelschlagel's death, my parents continued to be hounded by the SD. We were under constant surveillance and no longer felt safe, so the Dutch Resistance placed us in a safe house just outside the city. One day after the Liberation, we returned to our home in the southern part of Amsterdam, and I went back to the 1st Montessori School.

Picking Pockets of the Dead:
Hannie J. Ostendorf Voyles

In 1939, my sister Joosje and I started at the 1st Montessori School when we moved to the Old South neighborhood in Amsterdam. Because our parents were about to divorce, my mother had moved us to this new area. We lived on the Beethovenstraat, and my father moved nearby to the Cliostraat. Before that, we had been students at the 6th Montessori School with Anne Frank. Anne was older than I was; she was in the upper grades, but I remember seeing her at school and in the neighborhood.

Our new school was just around the corner from our house, and I joined the first grade class. I played with counting frames, and traced sandpaper letters until I could write them on my own. Other frames had laces on them and that's how I learned to button and lace my shoes. The learning was always practical, and the activities were fun to do.

When the war began, the adults were always nervous. Everyone was glued to the radio, and they frequently shook their heads in disbelief as they listened. For some reason, we had to cover our windows with black paper and our home became much darker.

I didn't understand what was happening, so I was always happy to go to school. I walked a considerable distance, some ten blocks, out of my way to pick up my best friend Olga, and we walked back to school together. My other good friend, Nancy Mesman, lived outside of town and when I was allowed to play at her house, I stayed overnight.

The recreation area in front of our school was very important to me, and I played hundreds of hours of soccer there. When I played by myself, I practiced bouncing the ball on my head over and over again, sometimes for hours. If there were two of us, we kicked the ball against the wall of the school. When more kids came, the game was on! We made goal posts by laying our coats on the ground, and when the ball was kicked high and landed on the roof, someone had to climb up the rain pipe to get it. Of course the school didn't allow us to do this, and it was challenging, not only because we had to watch out for the teachers, but also because bits of broken glass had been cemented to the roof, glued there on purpose to keep us kids away. Getting the ball was more important than risking a cut, so we braved the climb and the glass, retrieved the ball, and threw it back down. Sometimes the game would start again before you could get off the roof, and more than once, I was left to my own devices to get back down.

Then came the war, and my carefree childhood was shattered. Before this time, I never realized my parents had a mixed marriage; my mother was Jewish and my father was Catholic. Although they intended to divorce, my parents decided to postpone it because the war created so much uncertainty. My mother had to wear that yellow star on her clothing at all times, but because we were only half Jewish, my sister and I did not. We went to the Catholic church every Sunday and attended a catechism class every Wednesday afternoon—Mother saw to that—and she made sure we did our homework.

The Germans took everything they could from the Dutch people. They confiscated our bicycles, radios, iron, steel objects, and tools. Later, they took our blankets, as well. Food was scarce, so it was rationed, and we had to stand in long lines at the stores to get anything to eat. Everything was stripped from the Dutch people and used for the German war effort. Oh, how we hated the Nazis!

One afternoon, Joosje came home and told a story about a classmate of hers who had asked their class, "Is my nose really that big?" My sister and I didn't understand what he meant, and Mother explained that the Nazis characterized the Jews as having big noses, trying to make the rest of us dislike them. They hung posters of the devil all over the city, a picture of a grotesque, grimacing face with an exaggerated nose. The caption warned about the evil Jew, and created much fear in Amsterdam. Of course Mother was Jewish herself, but she took measures to appear less Jewish and dyed her hair blonde.

Over time, Jews were forbidden from participating in everyday activities. They couldn't visit public places or public buildings, couldn't hold their jobs, attend the university, or use public transportation. Non-Jews were forbidden from visiting their Jewish friends and could not go to a Jewish doctor. Everybody in the Netherlands had an identity card, but the Jews' cards were stamped with a large black "J." Soon the *razzias* began, and the Jews were herded together and deported to Eastern Europe. Non-Jews who were viewed as "Jew lovers" risked their own deportation, as well.

Things got even worse. In 1942, I went to my girlfriend's house on the Jan van Eijkstraat, so we could walk to school together. When I got to her front door, I saw it was ajar, so I pushed it open and went inside. To my horror, they were dead—the whole family. I ran all the way to school and pretended that all was well. I didn't say a word to anyone; I didn't dare. I couldn't call attention to myself because I was afraid that if I were questioned, my Jewish mother would be arrested. Later the Germans pulled a truck up to the house and took all their furniture, and shortly after that we went back ourselves to strip the windowsills, to take the doors off the cabinets, and to get their wooden shelves. We hacked the wood with a hammer and screwdriver, so we could burn it in a large can on our balcony to cook our little bits of frozen sugar beets. Like many memories I blocked from the war, the names of these family members were completely obliterated from my mind. When I later learned that the entire Pinkhof family had committed suicide in September 1942, I realized they were, in fact, the family I had discovered.

By now, we had to hide our mother. If the doorbell rang, we said she was not home. If the Nazis came to our door, which happened several times, we had to scramble to get her out of sight. The Nazis were so adamant that the Jews be suppressed that in 1943, they announced that Jewish women in mixed marriages could gain an "exempt" status—that is, they would be exempt from the rules placed upon Jews—but only if they submitted to sterilization. This, of course, would keep them from bringing more Jewish children in the world. My mother was faced with a wrenching decision. Should she cling to her right to bear children, or should she submit to this procedure, just to stay alive? Ultimately, she decided to risk both the danger of the operation and the loss of future children, in order to be able to care for my sister and me, the children she already had.

I remember that day well, although I was only nine years old. Mother took me by the hand and we walked the long way to the hospital together. We had to walk because, after all, she was not allowed on the streetcar. I was my mother's protector that day. She dared not go alone to present herself to the Germans who might change their minds and decide to deport her to a concentration camp. If she had a child with her, she thought they would be less likely to arrest her. After the operation, the cruel ripping out of her womb, we walked hand-in-hand back home.

When I wasn't at school, I played in the street with the neighborhood children. We often hunted for coal to fuel the stoves in our homes. We followed the German coal trucks, and when they stopped to unload, we crawled underneath and took as many pieces as we could fit in our hands and pockets. We learned to make little "bombs" by shoving gunpowder between a nut and a screw, and then tossed them at the Nazi soldiers, right at the base of their boots. When they heard the explosions that followed, they turned and drew their pistols in defense. We, of course, scattered like mice and disappeared into the streets we knew so well, leaving the soldiers red-faced and furious. It was a dangerous game, and one day I got caught. They took me to the nearby Gestapo headquarters and questioned me. The police demanded to know my address, and thinking quickly, I added 100 to our house number and gave them that false address. They threatened to come to my house to speak to my parents, and I feared they would do just that.

This whole adventure was a bad mistake on my part. Even though my mother had received an exemption, the situation for the Jews had gotten worse and she couldn't even go outside. She had no way of knowing where to find me, nor could she come looking for me. I couldn't even call her on the phone if I needed to because our telephone service had been cut some time ago.

Fortunately, I continued to have a reasonably normal school life. Of course, I got into trouble for writing and passing notes in class, but I also learned that I was responsible for my actions. When I joined our principal Mr. Eijgenstein's class, I found out I was not good at math, and I hated the story problems. I didn't care that if Train A left at one time and Train B left at another time, that I should be able to calculate the distance by using their arrival times. Why would anyone ever need to do that? My mother tried to tutor me, but despite her great patience, I usually ended up in tears.

Other activities were more interesting to me. I liked to go out in the early mornings to hunt for shrapnel after a night of air attacks. The Allied bombers would fly over the Netherlands on their way to bomb Germany, but the German anti-aircraft installations would try to shoot them down, leaving behind the fragments of shells. Sometimes they were still too hot to handle when I tried to pick them up. I saved my collection in a shoebox, and at school we traded them. If you found any shrapnel that still had copper pieces on them, those were better than the ordinary ones!

To the best of my memory, I think there was a time that the 1st Montessori School was closed for awhile. That may have been after the bombing of the Gestapo Headquarters, which was split between two separate high schools that were right across the street from one another, less than a quarter mile away. Who could ever forget that Sunday, November 26, 1944?

I sat in the window of our living room, on the second floor where I could see the school clock tower. It was just after 1:25 p.m. I called to my sister, "Come look, look—over there! Airplanes are flying down the street!" It was already too late to take cover; the British were attacking.

Bombs screamed through the air and exploded in the street. Machine gunfire rattled around us, as the Germans attempted to shoot down the bombers. We ran downstairs and stood by the front door, shaking. We couldn't believe we were being attacked. Shortly after the bombings, British fighter planes came back to gun down the German soldiers who were running in the street, away from the burning Gestapo Headquarters.

Then suddenly it was over! A muted, deadly quiet hung over the street. We could see very little; the debris and rubble formed a thick veil of dust, and the daylight turned dark.

Joosje and I went out to the street. Thousands of papers fluttered and danced through the air like confetti, and we chased after them, thinking they might be leaflets the BBC had dropped from the airplanes to deliver good news about the war. We were wrong. They were much more important than that. The "leaflets" were official documents from Gestapo headquarters, records for the final deportation of Amsterdam's Jews that was scheduled to take place the very next day. My own mother was a target of that deportation and had been ordered to report for immediate removal to a concentration camp. Those lost documents gave her yet one more chance to survive!

The view on the ground was much different from the confetti-filled sky. Dead bodies were everywhere: in the street, on the sidewalks, in doorways. Joosje and I scavenged through their pockets, hoping to find something of value, something that could help us survive yet another day. Some of the dead were people we knew. A dentist and his family, who lived on the corner and had just celebrated their anniversary that weekend, were among the dead. His dental tools covered the sidewalk, and we gathered them up and took them home. The Gestapo Headquarters at both the high schools were in flames. The clock on the tower had stopped and time stood still, frozen at 1:25 p.m. that entire winter.

A couple of days later when the fire trucks left the charred Headquarters, many of us children returned to pilfer whatever we could from the buildings. We took the wheels and frame from a stroller, strapped it with a belt, and entered the half-burned buildings to strip as much as we could from the furniture and other items. It was the beginning of the winter of 1944, and there was no more food. There was no electricity, no gas, no light, no heat. We were cold and we were hungry; we needed wood to burn for heat and to use as fuel to cook the few frozen sugar beets we had. We piled the pieces of wood on our impromptu wagon and used the belt as a lead to pull it home. We went back and forth, and back and forth to the burned-out schools, until we could no longer get in the buildings. On one of our trips, several of us went inside the gym. A large portrait of Hitler was mounted on the wall. We knew exactly what to do. We shouted, "ONE, TWO, THREE," then spit on his face!

We had been without food for so long that the whole city was starving. Once a week we received a ration card to exchange for half a loaf of bread and two potatoes per person, if they were available. The rations were for Friday only; the rest of the time the stores were closed since they had nothing to sell. Every Friday morning, I stood outside the bakery at 4:00 a.m. in sub-freezing temperatures. It was dark, it was very cold, and I had outgrown my clothes. If I was not among the first ten or twelve people in line, I wouldn't get any bread. The bakery opened at 8:00 a.m., but was completely sold out by 8:30. It was practically impossible for me not to eat the bread on the way home after standing in line for four hours.

We often dreamed of it, and the Liberation finally came on May 5, 1945—not a day too soon. The night before, we had heard rumors that the Canadians were nearing the city, so we went out in the street in spite of the curfew, singing, yelling, and whistling on our fingers. Our celebration ended abruptly when some German soldiers raised their guns and shot them in the air. We dispersed and ran for shelter, and the liberation came the next day.

The Dutch are a proud people who had lost too much—too many people, too many freedoms, too many possessions—yet, our strong spirits bound us together to resist the Nazi efforts and offer some safe havens for the Jews. But some in the Netherlands did the exact opposite; they not only supported the Nazis, they joined them in their practices and debased their own people. We knew who they were, and we did not forget what they had done. Within a week after the Liberation, the young women who had sympathized and fraternized with the Nazi soldiers—those foolish ones who had become their friends, lovers, confidantes, and sources of information—were captured by the Dutch Resistance and brought to the square in front of the 1st Montessori School for public humiliation. The entire community was involved in avenging their offenses, even the children. Kitchen chairs were brought to the square and the women were seated upon them. I remember my part. I helped the adults tie those women to the backs of the chairs so they couldn't get up and run away. Then I stepped back and watched as their hair was chopped off and their heads were shaved. Their shame now exposed, they covered their heads with scarves and avoided being seen in public.

Although we were liberated, we were far from being healed. My best friend Olga also managed to survive, and we were sent away to the southeastern part of the Netherlands to be fed by farmers and recuperate from our malnutrition. The southern half of the country had been liberated six months earlier, and food was more readily available there. We were among the hundreds of starving children who were sent elsewhere to recuperate from the physical effects of the war. Once we were properly nourished, we returned to our homes.

My parents picked up where they left off, and they finally got their divorce. My sister stayed with my mother in Amsterdam, and I moved with my father to Bussum, a small town about thirty-five miles from Amsterdam where I started Montessori high school. Just a few days after I graduated, I left the Netherlands with my mother and sister and emigrated to America in the early days of 1950.

THIS WAS THE DAY

This was the day.
The time had come.
Mother dressed carefully for the appointment
that would change her life.

Her style, her allure, would see her through.
She took my hand as we began our walk.

Surely, the doctor would recognize
that a woman of her bearing
with a child of nine by the hand
was not someone whose egg-carrying stalks
should be ripped out ...
One look at her and he would surely know ...
... yes, he'd see and help her ...

It was a long walk along familiar shops.
She held my hand which was unusual but
something was up ... she had explained it all ...
several times in fact:
If I went with her, they would not keep her.
They would remove her mother organs.
The Nazis would leave her alone:
She would be EXEMPT from deportation ...
because a woman who could no longer bear
Jewish children was no further threat to the Reich.

I sat very still and waited:
They would cut her and it would be over.

Years later I learned that it would never be over.

The Role of Our Teachers

Hiding Jewish Children:
Miss Jeanne Lindeman

When she was a brand-new teacher, Jeanne Lindeman provided a safe house for the most vulnerable of all, the very youngest Jewish children. Inez Keestra-Aussen was only two years old when Miss Lindeman brought her to the attic apartment in her parents' home where she lived. During the week while she was teaching, she placed Inez in other homes and on several occasions took her to a safe house in the country. On the weekends she took care of Inez herself. Arranging her care was a constant effort and, in 1942, after six months of shuffling the child back and forth, she finally found her a permanent home with a miner's family in the southeast. They agreed to raise the girl until the end of the war, which undoubtedly saved her life. Afterwards, Inez and her brother were reunited and went to live with their two aunts.

Miss Lindeman helped save other children, as well, but she never discussed these activities, not even with her future students when she taught them about the war years. One student from the 1960s remembered that when she talked about the war, rather than mention her own role in hiding Jewish children, she tried to explain the meaning of real hunger and the climate of starvation they all endured. She told her students that one time during the "hunger winter" of 1944, she was on her way to school when she witnessed an attack on a bread delivery cart. The desperate people had overturned it, and the precious bread, more valuable than gold, rolled down the street. The temptation was so great and her hunger so severe that she, too, scooped up a loaf and ran back home!

Then she shared a more gruesome memory. The Nazis were enraged after the Dutch Resistance had murdered two of their high-ranking SD officers, just blocks from the 1st Montessori School. To retaliate, they went back to the neighborhood that night and rounded up every man on the block between the ages of fifteen and fifty, marched them to the street, and shot them all. Afterwards, passers-by were forced to look at the dead. Even the children couldn't escape their faces.

Driven to the Attic:
The Principal, Wim F. Eijgenstein

Wim Eijgenstein became the principal of the 1st Montessori School in 1941. Like many of the Dutch who were moved by the plight of their countrymen, he was concerned about the wives of the Merchant Marines, the sailors who had set sail before the Nazis invaded but were forbidden to return when the war broke out. Their wives and families could not get ration cards to purchase food, and Mr. Eijgenstein helped secure them.

He also distributed the highly illegal Underground newspaper, *The Word*, which he reproduced on the school's duplicating machine.

Wim Eijenstein

Many parents tried to shield their children from their Underground activities, but they weren't often successful. Mr. Eijgenstein's son Pim remembered the first night his father didn't come home. Although he hadn't slept in his bed, his mother had messed up the sheets and blankets and told Pim that he had gone to school particularly early that morning. Even though she tried to fool him, the seven-year-old knew that his father had been away all night.

When the *razzias* to capture Dutch men intensified in 1943, Mr. Eijgenstein and one of his neighbors were forced to hide in the school. There was a storage area in the gym where they kept mats, and it had a trapdoor that led to a space large enough for the two men to share. Another time they hid in the school attic, which could only be reached by climbing a ladder and squeezing through a crawl space on the second floor. Though uncomfortable, the men were safe in the rafters and were never discovered, despite the Nazi searches. When the *razzia* was over, they returned to their normal activities.

Wim Eijgenstein was completely devoted to his students and, even after the Allied bombing damaged the school, he continued to hold classes in his office, although the rest of the school could not be used.

Traversing the Netherlands:
Mrs. Sini Broerse

At first, Gerrit Oorthuys did not attend the 1st Montessori School, but his mother Sini Broerse was a teacher there. She had earned her teaching credentials in 1931, and had planned to teach in an elementary school, preferably in a blue-collar neighborhood, but at the time there were few positions available. Gerrit's idealistic parents had become Socialists in their late twenties; his father was a photographer for the Dutch Communist Party. The year 1937 was significant for two reasons: Gerrit's sister Dorothe was born, and his parents got a divorce. His father's financial support for them was hopelessly inadequate, only one guilder per week—approximately 56 cents. His mother had to find work to support her children, so she went back to school to get her Montessori certificate and completed her student teaching at the 2nd Montessori School where Gerrit was a student.

In 1940, Sini quite unexpectedly got a full-time job at the 1st Montessori School in the affluent Old South neighborhood. Every morning she took six-year-old Gerrit to the streetcar and handed him over to the conductor, who made certain he got off at the stop by his school. She then biked over to 1st Montessori, carrying little Dorothe on the back, where she taught a class of first, second, and third graders.

After the divorce, the family had moved to 257 Prinsengracht, to a house that had extra rooms they could rent out. They were only a few doors away from The Annex at number 267 Prinsengracht, where Anne Frank and her family were in hiding. But Gerrit never knew the Frank family was there; so many things were kept from the children. He could see The Annex from his house, but he paid it no attention because his mother always kept their drapes closed.

They also hid Jews in their home—three to five at a time. Some of their guests stayed for just a day or two, like the writer Leo Meter and a Russian student named Jan Bool, both of whom were later captured. Because they were hiding Jews, the family tried to keep a low profile, but couldn't always avoid unexpected visits from the authorities. One time the police came for a Jewish boy named Flip, and although he managed to escape to the roof, he forgot to close the trapdoor and was arrested minutes later. He quickly slipped a piece of paper to Sini that she dropped in her pocket. The police officer saw this and demanded she hand it over, but Sini refused. He came near to her and said, "You disappoint me, ma'am," whereupon she promptly replied, "I won't tell you what disappoints me about you!" Ironically, the paper turned out to be a banknote to pay for Flip's rent.

The children rarely saw their father. He now worked for the Dutch Resistance and created false identity cards until May 1944, when he was arrested and sent to a work camp in Amersfoort. Sini pleaded for her ex-husband's release and spoke to one of his former photographer colleagues who, by this time, was a high ranking official in the SS. Remarkably, the officer was willing to help, and her former husband was released three months later.

By 1942, Sini was hiding so many people in their house that she sent Gerrit away to safety, to a family who lived in Kesteren in the middle of the country. The food was better there, and after some time Dorothe joined him. They stayed there for two years until Sini, encouraged by the Allied victory at Normandy, finally went to get her children.

They set off on a walking tour, bound for the castle Eerde in the eastern part of the Netherlands. Other children who had been sent to Kesteren accompanied them, and on the way they either camped out or asked farmers to let them sleep in their haystacks. When they arrived at Eerde a couple of days later, they joined a friend of Sini's who was also transporting a group of children. They named their group "The Happy Brigade" and they eventually walked all the way back to Amsterdam.

Gerrit, now eleven, transferred to the 1st Montessori School where his mother still taught. Sini and Dorothe continued to ride their bike to school, but Gerrit didn't have a bike, so he walked. Collecting and trading shrapnel was a common activity for children during the war, and Gerrit had a large collection. While he was walking to school on October 25, he saw that two villas on the corner of the Apollolane were engulfed in flames. There was another boy nearby who was looking for shrapnel. Puzzled, Gerrit asked, "Why are you looking for shrapnel here?"

"I'm not looking for shrapnel," he answered, "I'm looking for bullets." When Gerrit looked down, he saw that the fallen leaves were drenched in blood. The previous night, twenty-nine men had been rounded up and shot right on that spot, in response to the murder of the German commander of the SD, Herbert Oehlschlagel. When the boy told Gerrit what had happened, he lost all interest in finding shrapnel.

After the Allies bombed the SD headquarters, the 1st Montessori School was damaged and was forced to close. About a month later, just before Christmas, Sini took her children on yet another walking tour. They were headed for Marum, about 180 miles from Amsterdam, where their aunt and uncle lived in a church parsonage. Uncle Bram was the minister, and they lived in a large house. Sini hoped they had enough food to share.

Their departure from Amsterdam did not go well. Sini pushed a stroller packed with their personal items, but by the time they got about a mile from their house, one of the wheels came off. They went back to fix it, then set off again. Sini had managed to find a piece of bacon and some bread that she hid in the stroller with their other essentials, and Dorothe, now seven, was allowed to sit on top, particularly when they covered long distances.

Sini had meticulously planned their journey. The first day they got as far as Baarn, about thirty miles away. They stayed with an acquaintance of hers who shared his bed with Gerrit on one side and a Jewish boy he was hiding on the other. The next stretch took them to

Amersfoort, about seven miles further. Sini carried a little book full of addresses of "safe" teachers who offered their homes to those in need, and they spent the night in Amersfoort with one of them.

The next day, they walked twenty-five miles to Putten, where they couldn't help but notice that the entire population consisted of women. The Germans had conducted a *razzia* there to avenge an attack on two of their lieutenants and corporals. One of the lieutenants had died in the

Sini Broerse

skirmish. As a penalty, the Nazis sent all the men in Putten to the concentration camp at Neuengamme, near Hamburg, Germany. Of the 589 captured, only forty-nine ever returned.

On Christmas Day, the family walked thirty miles to Zwolle, and the following day they went another twelve miles to Staphorst, where they found beds to sleep in. There was one drawback: the beds were infested with fleas. Sini slathered petroleum jelly on their skin to ward off the bites, but the stench of it was overpowering. The next day they ended up sleeping in a cow barn in Meppel, only seven miles away. Here they actually saw several cars, a sight not seen in ages! Two days later they hitched a ride on a truck and crawled under the tarp to try to get warm. It was no use. The temperature was frigid and a lot of snow had fallen; they were, quite literally, freezing. On January 1, 1945, Sini and the children arrived at Groningen, and from there, they were taken to Marum.

Their aunt and uncle treated them well. Sini enrolled Gerrit and Dorothe in school and they played with the local children. Thankful to have a place to stay for a few months, the family remained at the parsonage until the end of the war. The Liberation in Marum was low-keyed compared to other areas of the Netherlands. The Nazis left quietly, and shortly thereafter the Canadian soldiers, who looked like they'd slept in their clothes for weeks, arrived without fanfare.

By the summer of 1945, it was time to go home. Sini said goodbye to her relatives and took her children to the harbor in Lemmer, in the northern province of Friesland. From there, they had to take a boat to reach the ferry that went to Amsterdam and, after the ferry ride, they finally returned home. By then, Gerrit was too old for the elementary school, but he needed a year to catch up so he could qualify for high school, so he was enrolled in a "6A" class. Sini and Dorothe went back to the 1st Montessori School.

Shortly after the Liberation, a faculty meeting that included a number of schools was called to discuss the loss of children. Mr. Eijgenstein, the principal of the 1st Montessori School, told the group that a large number of his students had not returned from the concentration camps, and a teacher from a nearby school said he had lost an even greater number of students. The meeting was completely silenced when a teacher from a school in the Nieuwe Kerkstraat reported that not one single child from his school had returned.

Sini was completely devoted to her work both before and after the war, and she was much appreciated by her colleagues and students as an enterprising educator. After tramping around the Netherlands, one would think she would be tired of walking, but that wasn't the case. She created interesting excursions and took her students on long walks to the beach and to the youth hostel in the nearby dunes. Her political opinions changed after the war, and she lost faith in communism when she learned that Stalin had participated in the horrors. Years later, she joined the Labor Party.

In 1972, Sini retired from the 1st Montessori School. As one might imagine, she stayed very active in her retirement and eventually returned to the school to teach folk dancing.

Sini Broerse died in 1998.

Our Fallen Heroes

RAF Pilot:
Daniel Sajet

Daan Sajet was a student at the 1st Montessori School when he was young, and he graduated from high school in August 1940, just a few months after the Nazis invaded the Netherlands. Daan was an energetic and athletic young man, and a few days after his graduation, he told his parents he was going sailing with a friend. His parents agreed that the boys had earned an afternoon of fun since they had worked hard and finished their schooling. The boys set off and they never saw Daan again.

Daan Sajet in his RAF uniform

It wasn't the first time that Daan had disappeared. Earlier he had tried to escape to France to join the Dutch army that was stationed there, but the Nazis intercepted him and sent him home. This time Daan was successful. The boys sailed across the North Sea to England, quite a risky endeavor considering the number of German patrol boats that were on the lookout for such activity.

Back in the Netherlands, the political climate grew more menacing. In February, a general strike resulted in the arrest of all the city council members. Daan's father, Dr. Sajet, escaped the *razzia* by slipping through the back door just as the SD came through the front. He went to a nearby safe house, and from there he traveled to the Veluwe, a forested area about sixty-five miles east of Amsterdam. Several weeks later, he heard that it was safe to go back home, but from that time forward his medical practice was limited to Jews only.

The writing was on the wall; Dr. Sajet knew things would only get worse and that he had to find a way to escape with his wife and other children. They located a rowboat and left from Petten on the northwest coast of Holland. The whole family took turns rowing, and after thirty-six hours, they reached Lowestoft on the coast of England.

Through a Dutch friend who had already emigrated to England, they made contact with one of the Dutch Ministers who was in exile and learned that Daan had joined the Royal Air Force. While he was in training to earn his wings, his airplane had crashed—on June 16, his mother's birthday. Daan lived only one day and was cremated on June 20, 1941.

Dutch Resistance Fighters:
Sape and Bram Kuiper

Former 1st Montessori School brothers Sape and Bram Kuiper were fighters in the Dutch Resistance, and they were active in a group that met at #6 Corellistraat, a house across the street from the 1st Montessori School. Sape was aggressive, and on his eighteenth birthday—January 25, 1943—he set fire to the Rembrandt Theatre where the Germans showed their propaganda films, and it burned to the ground.

Two months later he shot a police inspector, and then on July 22, 1943, Sape killed a dentist who was an informant for the Gestapo who had turned in his Jewish patients who were in hiding. After the assault, Sape fled the scene on his bicycle, but a window washer thought he was a bicycle thief and threw his ladder on top of Sape to capture him. When he realized the bike belonged to Sape, he let him go.

Headstones in Overveen

The Secret Police would have relished that capture. They were determined to conquer the Dutch Resistance, so they took over a Jewish boarding house at #16 Corellistraat, just a few doors away from where their group met. From that location, the Nazis monitored their activities, and shortly thereafter they arrested them all. Sape Kuiper was executed in Amsterdam, and Bram Kuiper and the other members were shot to death in the dunes of Overveen, where they were all buried. To recognize his valor during the Nazi occupation, the Sape Kuiper Center in Amsterdam is named in honor of this fallen hero.

Killed After the War Ended:
Willem Zeeman

For the Dutch, the war ended on May 5, 1945, at 8:00 a.m. Two days later, a fierce battle erupted while many Dutch citizens celebrated their new freedom on the central square of Amsterdam. For unknown reasons, German soldiers fired directly into the crowd of partying people. Twenty people died, and 120 others were wounded. Immediately after that, another band of Germans started shooting at random, trying to clear a path to the train station where they would escape. When they arrived, they were surprised to find that the Dutch Resistance had already commandeered the station and was systematically stripping the Nazi soldiers of their weapons. A battle ensued between the Resistance and the fleeing Germans.

Willem H. Zeeman, age 22, was a sergeant in the Dutch Resistance. He had taken his position in the baggage area where he aggressively fought the remaining Germans. He had already killed several but, unfortunately, one of them maneuvered from behind and shot Willem dead. An hour later the battle ended. Seventeen Germans had been killed, and an unknown number were wounded.

On May 8, 1945, the Canadians arrived in Amsterdam and met their glorious welcome as they crossed the Berlage Bridge on the south side of the city. Thousands and thousands of citizens gave the soldiers a heartfelt and emotional welcome, and Willem should have been one of them.

Epitaph for Willem Zeeman

Willem Zeeman was the grandson of Nobel prizewinner Pieter Zeeman (physicist, 1865-

1943), yet he was honored in his own right for his dedicated role in the Dutch Resistance and his ultimate sacrifice for the cause. He was posthumously honored as a hero and was awarded The Bronze Cross for continuing the fight against the Nazis, even though the war had officially ended two days before.

The Murdered Ones

The Search Into Our Past

On May 11, 2001, we celebrated the 75th birthday of the 1st Montessori School, and all of our former students were invited to the reunion. Jaap Post, a former student born in 1925, asked the key question that planted the seed for this book. He wanted to know which of the school's Jewish students had died during the Second World War.

It was a great question. We only knew about a few students whose names were included in a notice received after the war, but a serious investigation had never been launched. Only after the book *In Memoriam* was published—a book that listed all 107,000 Dutch-Jewish victims—was it possible to search for our students. Our investigation was intensive, but we found no more than ten names. We later learned that the book was not comprehensive; it did not include the names of all who had perished, and it contained numerous errors, as well.

So we turned to the Internet and decided to start over, to start at the beginning. Jaap Post offered to track the nine hundred students who had been registered at the school between 1926 and 1945, and to compare those names to the ones listed on the official website of Dutch Jewry. More than a year later, he had found the names of forty-nine of our children in the database. For many reasons we had to put this work aside, and two years passed before we returned to it.

In June 2004, when we spoke to a former teacher about some pictures we'd found in our archives, she urged us to immediately contact the other former teachers while we still had time. The teachers were growing old, and some of them had already died. If we wanted to learn about their experiences at the 1st Montessori School—as well as the names of both the children and their teaching colleagues—we had better make haste. The spark was ignited and Jaap Post's work was resurrected.

In the meantime, Yad Vashem—the world center for documentation, research, education, and commemoration of the Holocaust—had expanded its database to include the names of all victims of WWII, which allowed us to search for the names of children we hadn't yet found. After two months we completed the task and our list of victims grew to sixty.

In 2004, we were searching through the school archives for an old photograph when we stumbled upon the registration book for the kindergarten class. It dawned on us that when the 1st Montessori School was started in 1925, many children who had attended our kindergarten were sent to different elementary schools after that. We had not thought to include their names in our previous research, and we should have. Our project expanded, and we were now in a hurry because our 75th anniversary celebration was coming up, when we would present a Memory Plaque that listed the names of all the children who had died. Invitations to the dedication were sent to all of our former students, and we particularly hoped that those who had been students during the war years would attend.

Within two months, we tracked down another 1,300 students found in the kindergarten registration book and added ninety-one names to our list of victims. That summer, we received yet another name from the Swedish government, and in the fall of 2005, we consulted two additional websites—joodsmonument.nl and kampwesterbok.nl— where we identified three more students. Some of our female students had been officially listed under their married names, and from that information, nine more names were added to the list. Although we explored every avenue, we could not find any information regarding five of our students who had been sent to a JEWS ONLY school in September 1941.

Ultimately, our research concluded that 173 former students from the 1st Montessori School were murdered by the Nazis during WWII, and their names are etched on the Memory Plaque that was dedicated in 2006. Most of them were killed in gas chambers the same day they arrived at the concentration camps. A number of them lived for several months and then succumbed to exhaustion. Some children were forced to march long distances to work on the land or to move to another camp. They were often clubbed to death along the way; some died from disease. When we could not determine the exact day they died, we recorded the last day of the month they were still living, as their date of death.

They were our children, and we honor them all.

Rollbook of the Dead

The Nazis murdered 173 former pupils from the 1st Montessori School during WWII. Their names are etched on the Memory Plaque at the school.

Family Name	Names	Died	At	Age
Abrahams	Maurits	1943-07-02	Sobibor	13 years
Acathan	Dorothea Helena	1942-10-08	Auschwitz	6 years
Adler	Anita Hendrika	1943-03-05	Sobibor	17 years
Adler	Marie	1943-03-05	Sobibor	15 years
Adler	Elkan	1944-1945	Vermist	13-14 years
Akker	Yvonne	1943-06-04	Sobibor	18 years
Arenson	Gustav Louis	1944-10-06	Auschwitz	12 years
Asscher	Salomon	1945-03-01	Bergen-Belsen	15 years
Asscher	Isaac	1945-04-01	Bergen-Belsen	17 years
Asscher	Jacob	1945-04-01	Bergen-Belsen	14 years
Bed	Philip Jean	1945-04-06	Bergen-Belsen	11 years
Bed	John	1942-09-30	Auschwitz	16 years
Beek	Leo Simon	1943-05-14	Sobibor	17 years
Beem, van	Marianna Mathilda	1943-02-12	Auschwitz	13 years
Berlijn	Johanna Isabella	1943-07-09	Sobibor	24 years
Blindeman	Emanuel	1943-07-02	Sobibor	8 years
Blindeman	Gonda	1943-07-02	Sobibor	13 years
Blitz	Madeleine Sonja	1942-08-24	Auschwitz	9 years
Bouwman	Henri Maurice	1945-05-31	Bergen-Belsen	20 years
Braun	Maurice	1943-09-03	Auschwitz	14 years
Braunberger	Dennis Julius	1942-08-13	Auschwitz	7 years
Braunberger	Marcel Dé	1942-08-13	Auschwitz	10 years
Breemer	Carla	1942-09-17	Auschwitz	13 years
Brouwer	Sydney Arthur	1942-09-14	Auschwitz	21 years
Carow	Marga Grete	1944-10-25	Auschwitz	14 years

Family Name	Names	Died	At	Age
Cohen	Louis	1942-09-30	Auschwitz	19 years
Cohen	Joseph Elias	1943-06-04	Sobibor	9 years
Cohen	Samuel Abraham	1943-06-04	Sobibor	11 years
Cohen	Alexander Bernhard	1943-06-04	Sobibor	11 years
Cohen	Marianne Louise	1943-06-04	Sobibor	14 years
Cohen	Johanna Rosetta	1943-08-27	Auschwitz	11 years
Cornalijnslijper	Jonas Ephraim	1942-08-11	Auschwitz	16 years
Dam, van	Hans Arnoud	1944-02-11	Auschwitz	10 years
Dam, van	Frederika	1943-07-09	Sobibor	13 years
Deen	Henri	1942-09-21	Auschwitz	17 years
Dreijer	Inge	1943-05-28	Sobibor	16 years
Dreijer	Hans	1943-05-28	Sobibor	14 years
Dresden	Bart	1942-08-12	Auschwitz	6 years
Duizend	Harold Lodewijk	1943-07-02	Sobibor	12 years
Duizend	Paul Robert	1943-07-02	Sobibor	12 years
Eigenfeld	Leo Bernard	1942-09-21	Monowitz	11 years
Eigenfeld	Karla	1942-09-21	Monowitz	13 years
Emmering	Jacques	1943-07-23	Sobibor	13 years
Emmering	Arnold	1943-07-23	Sobibor	15 years
Englander	Dora	1943-04-02	Sobibor	18 years
Esso, van	Leonard Samuel	1943-03-05	Sobibor	6 years
Flesseman	Marius Leendert Carol	1943-02-14	Auschwitz	11 years
Forstenzer	Jacob Abraham	1943-07-23	Sobibor	8 years
Fortenzer	Johannes Peter	1943-07-23	Sobibor	16 years
Fraenkel	Liane Isobel	1943-07-16	Sobibor	7 years
Frank	Esther	1943-07-16	Sobibor	13 years
Frank	Philip Joachim Aron	1943-07-16	Sobibor	8 years
Gelder, van	Marion Eva	1942-07-24	Auschwitz	21 years
Gelder, van	Judith	1943-02-12	Auschwitz	16 years
Gelder, van	Anna	1943-07-16	Sobibor	23 years
Gelder, van	Renée	1943-07-16	Sobibor	23 years
Gersons	Peter	1943-07-09	Sobibor	8 years

Family Name	Names	Died	At	Age
Gobets	Hetty Marguérite	1943-11-30	Sobibor	22 years
Godschalk	Marianne Helena	1943-07-23	Sobibor	15 years
Goede, de	Salomon	1942-08-11	Auschwitz	16 years
Goede, de	Jacques	1945-03-15	Centraal Europa	16 years
Gokkes	David Jacob	1943-02-05	Auschwitz	14 years
Goldsteen	Siegfried	1944-06-30	Centraal Europa	21 years
Grünberg	Margot	1943-04-16	Sobibor	14 years
Grünfeld	Charles Schemanjahn	1944-10-01	Auschwitz	16 years
Halle	Robert Hans	1942-08-09	Auschwitz	11 years
Helmstadt	Joost Max Gerard	1943-06-11	Sobibor	19 years
Henriques de la Fuente	Margaretha	1942-09-30	Auschwitz	19 years
Henriques de la Fuente	Benvenida	1943-07-16	Sobibor	21 years
Herpen, van	Maurits Abram Roger	1943-05-21	Sobibor	15 years
Hertzberger	Philip Ivan	1942-10-05	Auschwitz	14 years
Hirschel	Frederika Maria	1943-01-13	Auschwitz	19 years
Hoek	Justus	1945-03-08	Apeldoorn	17 years
Hoek	Rini Elisa	1922-02-16	Sobibor	21 years
Huiden, van	Josephine Rozetta	1943-07-02	Sobibor	18 years
Jong, de	Emma Jacoba	1943-06-04	Sobibor	13 years
Jongh, de	Maximiliaan Samuel	1945-04-10	Bergen-Belsen	9 years
Kahn	Bernhard	1945-02-27	Bergen-Belsen	17 years
Kan	Daniël	1944-10-12	Auschwitz	12 years
Ketellapper	Josine Henriëtte	1943-07-09	Sobibor	17 years
Keijser	Anna Jacqueline	1942-08-10	Auschwitz	10 years
Kisch	Hans Alfred	1943-09-03	Auschwitz	9 years
Klein	Gerda Sophie	1944-03-06	Auschwitz	9 years
Kloots	Isabella	1942-10-11	Monowitz	10 years
Kloots	Sem Jacques	1942-10-11	Monowitz	13 years
Kohlmann	Irmgard	1943-11-19	Auschwitz	15 years

Family Name	Names	Died	At	Age
Kolthoff	Jakob Willem Benedictus	1943-06-11	Sobibor	9 years
Kolthoff	Selly Henderika	1943-06-11	Sobibor	7 years
Konijn	Eduard	1942-09-30	Auschwitz	22 years
Koster	Mathilde	1942-09-14	Auschwitz	12 years
Koster	Meijer	1942-09-14	Auschwitz	14 years
Kous, van der	Joseph Jules	1942-11-09	Auschwitz	10 years
Kous, van der	Meijer Joseph	1942-11-09	Auschwitz	13 years
Kuiper	Abraham Kornelis	1943-10-23	Overveen	21 years
Kuiper	Sape	1943-10-01	Overveen	19 years
Laan, van der	Eliza	1944-01-28	Auschwitz	20 years
Landau	Estera	1943-10-31	Auschwitz	16 years
Levison	Helena	1943-07-02	Sobibor	24 years
Levy	Renée Ketty	1942-09-21	Auschwitz	9 years
Levy-van Beets	Marion Helene	1943-07-16	Sobibor	19 years
Ligtenstein	Max	1945-02-16	Bergen-Belsen	17 years
Limburg	Pauline	1943-04-09	Sobibor	12 years
Lissaur	Engelina Margarete Carrie	1945-06-04	Landskrona	14 years
Locher	Hartog	1943-07-02	Sobibor	7 years
Lustig	Ilse Ruth	1943-08-27	Auschwitz	12 years
Malkindsohn	Inge	1942-09-10	Auschwitz	14 years
Manheim	Catherine	1942-08-12	Auschwitz	10 years
Markus	Ralph	1943-02-12	Auschwitz	14 years
Meents	Louis Jacques	1942-09-17	Auschwitz	11 years
Mendes	Alfred	1943-07-02	Sobibor	12 years
Moppes, van	Greta Clara	1942-09-14	Auschwitz	7 years
Nunes Cardozo	Maurits Paul	1944-03-31	Auschwitz	20 years
Nunes Cardozo	Marcelle Simone	1943-11-30	Auschwitz	18 years
Nol	Mozes Richard	1943-11-19	Auschwitz	23 years
Odewald	Herman Rudolf	1944-02-11	Auschwitz	10 years
Oettinger	Elinor	1944-10-18	Auschwitz	15 years
Oostra	Evaline Catharina	1943-05-28	Sobibor	16 years
Oppenheimer	Inge	1943-05-28	Sobibor	12 years
Pinkhof	Herman	1942-09-17	Amsterdam	14 years
Pinkhof	Rebecca Roza	1942-09-17	Amsterdam	12 years

Family Name	Names	Died	At	Age
Pinkhof	Adèle Sophie	1942-09-17	Amsterdam	10 years
Pinkhof	Jiska	1943-07-23	Sobibor	10 years
Pinkhof	Pinkas	1943-07-23	Sobibor	8 years
Pinkhof	Menachemja	1943-07-23	Sobibor	8 years
Polak	Herman	1945-03-02	Dachau	20 years
Polak	Esther	1943-11-19	Auschwitz	23 years
Polak	Louise	1943-11-19	Auschwitz	16 years
Polak	Nathan	1944-03-31	Auschwitz	20 years
Porcelijn	Helen Eveline	1943-07-02	Sobibor	14 years
Praag Sigaar, van	Herman Jacques	1942-11-05	Auschwitz	11 years
Praag Sigaar, van	Nanette	1942-11-05	Auschwitz	13 years
Praag, van	Samuel Herman Robert	1943-07-16	Sobibor	8 years
Prins	Ina	1943-06-11	Sobibor	12 years
Randerath	Anita Martha	1942-07-12	Auschwitz	7 years
Rine	Millie Louise	1944-03-06	Auschwitz	14 years
Roselaar	Julia Willy	1943-07-09	Sobibor	11 years
Roselaar	Salomon	1945-02-08	Bergen-Belsen	21 years
Sajet	Daniël	1941-06-17	London	21 years
Santcross	Henri Jacques	1945-05-23	Riesa	10 years
Serlui	Ruth	1943-07-02	Sobibor	10 years
Serlui	Johanna Elisabeth	1943-07-02	Sobibor	12 years
Serlui	Samuel	1943-07-02	Auschwitz	15 years
Serlui	Samuel	1943-07-23	Sobibor	12 years
Simon	Peter Rafael	1944-03-31		16 years
Simons	Robert Edouard	1945-05-15	Tröbitz	18 years
Speijer	Esther Helena	1943-07-09	Sobibor	12 years
Speijer	Max	1944-03-31	Polen	19 years
Spier	Jenny Trui	1942-10-27	Auschwitz	13 years
Spitz	Marcel	1943-07-09	Sobibor	24 years
Stenszewski	Louise Marte Renate	1943-09-07	Sobibor	15 years
Susan	Felix Mark	1943-11-19	Auschwitz	10 years
Teixeira de Mattos	Erica Raphaele	1944-10-15	Auschwitz	13 years
Thijn, van	Rebecca Hanna	1943-04-09	Sobibor	17 years

Family Name	Names	Died	At	Age
Tijn, van	Henri Jacob	1941-09-16	Mauthausen	18 years
Tijn, van	Frits Meijer	1944-05-01	Auschwitz	18 years
Vecht	Milly Frederika	1944-03-15	Auschwitz	22 years
Vecht	Martin Herman	1944-03-30	Auschwitz	20 years
Vecht	Jacob Henri	1944-07-31	Auschwitz	18 years
Verduin	Wanda	1944-02-15	Auschwitz	18 years
Verständig	Hannelore	1943-03-02	Auschwitz	6 years
Vleeschhouwer	Liesbeth	1945-05-13	Riesa	15 years
Vomberg	Clara Selma Martha	1943-07-23	Sobibor	8 years
Vries, de	Sal	1943-07-17	Sobibor	12 years
Waagenaar	Bernhard Chaim	1944-01-28	Auschwitz	7 years
Waagenaar	Joseph Barent	1944-01-28	Auschwitz	9 years
Waterman	Philip	1944-02-11	Auschwitz	12 years
Weinberg	Walter	1944-06-10	Auschwitz	13 years
Weinberg	Margrit	1944-06-10	Auschwitz	15 years
Wezel, van	Nanna	1943-10-31	Sobibor	17 years
Wijnschenk	Kitty	1943-05-14	Sobibor	14 years
Wolff	Ariel	1943-06-11	Sobibor	7 years
Wolfsbergen	Henriëtte Betsy	1944-02-11	Auschwitz	16 years
Zeeman	Willem Hendrik	1945-05-07	Amsterdam	22 years

Epilogue

Ronald Sanders, Author

This work could not have been accomplished without the contributions from students and teachers alike. Many people worked hard to make this book possible, and they offered many helpful ideas.

When the war started, about 20 percent of our students were Jewish. After the war, fewer than ten students came back to the 1st Montessori School; the Nazis had murdered more than 90 percent of the Jewish population of the Netherlands. Every child who lived through the war has his or her own story, and many of these stories ended up in this book.

It took hundreds of hours of research to prepare the list of victims: we studied pictures, we talked to relatives and classmates of the victims, and we reviewed their backgrounds. The stacks of documents that were produced left me completely overwhelmed by the enormity of this tragedy. I was moved to grief by what I learned about our children, like little Gerda Sophie Klein who started preschool on August 21, 1940. In September 1941, she was moved to a JEWS ONLY school, and three years later—on March 6, 1944—she was put on a transport to Auschwitz. There, she was gassed on her ninth birthday.

After the Liberation, life was still not easy for the children. Food and goods were scarce. Parents and children struggled to cope with the traumas of war. There was no support for the mental stress or emotional exhaustion the people experienced. The children of Nazi sympathizers had a very difficult time at school, too; they were teased and bullied, or altogether ignored.

It was a time we can never forget and should not ignore, when a soul-sickness passed over the world and damaged the lives of millions.

♦ ♦ ♦

Ronald Sanders teaches at the 1st Montessori School in Amsterdam, the Netherlands. He was raised in a Montessori environment and attended a Montessori school himself as a youngster, so it is no surprise that he would become a principal for eleven years, or that he would return to the classroom to work directly with young students.

Sanders' interests extend far beyond the classroom. He is drawn to philosophy, history, all types of music, and the local field hockey club. He plays the piano and likes taking long walks and bike rides. He and his wife also work in their garden—when time permits.

Ronald Sanders is dedicated to his students, and he has made our insight and understanding of the children of war possible.

Hannie J. Voyles,
Translator and Contributor

Hannie J. Ostendorf Voyles was born and raised in the Netherlands. Immediately after the war, she matriculated to the Montessori High School and then emigrated to the United States after graduation.

Hannie continued her education in California and Colorado, specializing in English and Linguistics. As a college teacher in Northern California, she realized that her students lacked exposure to the world. She immediately began to organize study tours for them and conducted some twenty tours for college students and their families. When Hannie learned that her college lacked a field hockey team, she taught the class herself, created and coached the team, and ultimately won seven league championships, as well as the state championship in 1978.

In 1995, during the 50-year commemoration of the Holocaust, she played a key role in bringing Miep Gies—who was instrumental in hiding Anne Frank and her family—to Chico, California, to attend the opening performance of *The Diary of Anne Frank*, presented by the Performing Arts department of her college.

Hannie Voyles is a go-getter whose philosophy is "Let's do what needs doing," and she frequently reaches for pen and paper to jot down a quick thought or a good idea. She created a "senior college" to keep older people involved and engaged, and she teaches them to write their personal histories, memoirs, and their "tales that need telling." The book, *Under the Big Top*, presents forty-five stories written by these seniors.

Hannie's energy reaches all around her, and she grounds herself by practicing Tai Chi, before or after her daily four- to five-mile walk and her regular game of golf. She has traveled a good bit of the world and encourages everyone to do the same.

For Discussion

1. Select one of the stories in the book and explain how reading it affected you.

2. If you could meet one of the people—a child or an adult—in this book, who would it be and what would you ask him/her? What else would you want to know about them?

3. These stories show how the children survived during the war years. Pick one of the stories to tell about a similar experience or emotion you felt as a child.

4. The book includes stories of betrayal. Who were betrayed and why? Can you relate to the victim? The betrayer?

5. Imagine yourself as one of these children. Who would that be and why? What advice would you give to that child?

6. How do you think the children coped with what they had endured? How were the rest of their lives affected by their childhood experiences during the war?

7. Many of these stories include children who were sent away to safety. What do you think their parents felt as they made this decision, and what motivated them to do so?

8. Is morality a principle that can be maintained during a war? Why or why not?

9. Do you know of other places in the world where similar conditions/ situations exist now?

10. Relate "bullying" as you know it to what you have read. Are there any similarities?

11. How should those kinds of aggressive actions be addressed? Are they natural, taught, or learned?

12. Racial, religious, political, and even historic differences set people apart. How does that apply to society today?

13. Compare and contrast the academic requirements for students in the Netherlands (p. 68) with students in your country.

The following poem was written by the students of Hank Marsh Jr. High School in Chico, California in response to a presentation by Hannie J. Voyles about living in Amsterdam during the Nazi occupation.

HANNIE'S "I AM FROM......"

I am from a Catholic dad and a Jewish mom,
from no smiles, no waving, no crying ...

I come from the innocence of Montessori schooldays,
playing field hockey and soccer beneath sunny Dutch skies.

I am from my mother's survival, hidden from view,
wrapped hastily in bed sheets as soldiers marched by.

I come from truckloads of neighbors, classmates, and friends torn
from their homes in the darkness of day and night.

I am from the age of silence and lost childhood,
forbidden to speak, Don't talk, Don't tell.

I come from nuts-and-bolts bombs and the trading of shrapnel and
messages of freedom concealed in BBC bandages.

I am from the feelings of helplessness, anger, and loss,
the endless pain, my eyes flushed with heartache and guilt.

I come from the blood of children who needlessly died.
Memories encased in the red stone worn around my neck.

I am from the bread and potatoes of day-to-day life
to the bittersweet chocolate of liberation and hope.

Recommended Reading

Books:

I Will Plant You a Lilac Tree: A Memoir of a Schindler's List Survivor, by Laura Hillman. Atheneum Books for Young Readers. 2005.

A Woman in Amber: Healing the Trauma of War and Exile, by Agate Nesaule. Penguin Books, 1997.

Too Small to Matter, by Edith Elefant. Traford Publishing, 2004.

Sky (A True Story of Courage During World War II), by Hanneke Ippisch. Scholastic Inc., 2007.

On Hitler's Mountain: Overcoming the Legacy of a Nazi Childhood, by Irmgard A. Hunt. HarperCollins, 2005.

The Hiding Place, by John Sherrill, Elisabeth Sherrill, and Corrie ten Boom. Chosen Books, 2006.

Video:

The Children of Fate: Voices from the War Years 1940 through 1945. Produced and directed by Carol L. Hardy, Hannie J. Voyles, and Donna Crowe.

CPSIA information can be obtained at www.ICGtesting.com/
Printed in the USA
LVOW101506051011

249244LV00003B/13/P